A Writer's Guide to Armed Professions

by
Clayton J. Callahan

Cover art by Peter Saga

This book has been reviewed by the US Department of Defense Office of Prepublication and Security Review, case number: DOPSR #14-S-0558, and cleared for publication as amended.

This book is dedicated to the memory of:

Spc. David Hickman

Last American soldier killed in Operation New Dawn (Iraq, November 2011).

DISCLAIMERS

Within these pages I make general references to US law as it applies to police officers. Please be aware, the author of this book is not a lawyer. Nothing in these pages constitutes "legal advice." This book is merely presenting guidelines to aid in the writing of realistic fiction, nothing more.

I have served as a US Army Counterintelligence Special Agent (MOS 35-L) and as such must walk a fine line. Nothing you read in this book will fall under the category of "classified" information under the National Security act of 1947, Title 18 of the US Code or the Uniform Code of Military Justice.

* * *

INTRODUCTION

For the writer who's never served in the military, worked in law enforcement or been involved in espionage in any way…this book was written for you.

To be fair, it's a primer. However, a primer is often the best way to start with any new subject. Sure, most folks have seen military movies and whatnot, but often references are dropped so casually or fast that many people just assume they understand what's going on. This works fine for the audience perhaps, or the reader—but for the author? No. For the author it can be minefield of misconceptions that may explode on your page at any moment.

This book is meant to give that writer a firm foundation in the history, structure, and culture of the armed professions. Basic questions are answered like: *Who gets saluted and why? When can a policeman use deadly force? What evidence does a detective need before she can make an arrest? What are some of the methods of espionage? And, why can't the CIA operate inside the United States?*

I have spent my adult life working in these diverse professions, and within these pages I share that experience with you—writer to writer. I also point you toward other good sources to deepen your knowledge on these subjects.

This book is divided into Parts A, B and C (military, police, and intelligence). Each section starts with historical background and progresses to a modern understanding of the profession involved.

So let's get started, shall we? After all, we have a lot of ground to cover…

PART A: THE MILITARY

CHAPTER I: ANCIENT MILITARY HISTORY

Understanding the past is the key to understanding the present. If your story takes place in modern times, great; but to write realistic military fiction, it helps to have some understanding of military history.

Also, modern soldiers are expected to know a bit of it. This is especially true for officers who graduated from a military academy, such as West Point, Annapolis or the Air Force Academy.

General Patton, of World War II fame, was especially fond of citing history. Interestingly, Patton also believed he was a reincarnated warrior who had fought for ancient Carthage against Rome. Yep, he was a character.

ANCIENT ARMIES

Arguably, the greatest of the ancient armies belonged to the Romans. For over

1,000 years, the Romans ruled an empire that stretched from Spain to Syria. Few other ancient civilizations could boast of such time and space. The Romans exerted a huge influence on later western armies and, in turn, the armies of the world. How did they do it? Put simply, they possessed an unstoppable military machine, the "legion."

Depending on the specific time and place in Rome's history, each legion contained about 6,000 troops. The legions were numbered, not named (The Tenth Legion, for example, or the Third).

The average soldier was called a "legionnaire." Roman Legions were sub-divided into cohorts, which were further divided into centuries (units of 100 men). A century was led by a noble called a "centurion" whose family essentially bought him the job. The noble's family typically trained the centurion in the arts of war since childhood. After a few years of breaking in, the centurion was either a pretty good leader or dead.

The centurion was the most junior of officers in the legion, but he still wielded great power over his troops. When legionnaires disobeyed orders, he decided their punishment, which could range from a flogging to execution. In extreme cases a Roman century could be "decimated" by its commander; that is to say, every tenth man would be executed.

The Romans generally relied on volunteers for the legions but also conscripted their citizens in times of need. Naturally, the draft was not a popular idea even then. For example, during the Punic Wars, young men of Rome would sometimes cut off their right thumb (making them unfit for service since they couldn't hold a sword).

The typical volunteer legionnaire served for a sixteen-year enlistment during the Republic period which was extended to twenty years under Cesar Augustus. Throughout the soldier's career, the legion provided all he needed from his food to his sandals, his armor, and his sword. However, the legionnaire was not paid much. Any extra money he got, he earned the old-fashioned way…he stole it from people he conquered. Thus, the legionnaire had a great incentive to go to war—loot!

Looting the town or city one attacked was an accepted practice of the time, and any farm between a marching legion and its target was fair game. One can easily imagine relationships between soldiers and civilians could be a bit strained.

When his service years were up, the legionnaire could either walk back to Rome or accept a farm in the conquered lands to settle down in. This kept large Roman veteran groups in frontier areas to help keep conquered peoples loyal. It also was the first time a society systematically rewarded military service with any kind of a pension.

The Roman legions used very specific tactics (methods of fighting). They were masters of hand-to-hand combat but not in the way of karate masters. The black belt fights alone, but the legionnaire fought in a group. Each Roman stood shoulder-to-shoulder with his comrades as he marched into battle. This way, a soldier only needed to worry about killing the enemy who stood exactly in front of him. If a foe moved to his left or right (his flanks) the legionnaire's comrade would kill that enemy for him. Ideally, the individual Roman legionnaire would never have to worry about being attacked from the flank, as he knew his buddies would protect him, just as he protected his buddies.

Soldiers are often said to "stand shoulder-to-shoulder" against a common foe, even though they do no such literal thing in battle today. A soldier must trust that his buddy will do his job well, so he can worry about his own part of the fight. This reliance on each other forms strong bonds of camaraderie. The flip side of that camaraderie is troops often deal harshly with a soldier who shows he can't perform or is somehow untrustworthy.

For a good quick reference on Rome, I recommend the *Osprey: Men at Arms series-Roman Centurions 31 BC-AD 500 or Republican Roman Army 200–104 BC*. Keep in mind things did change over the course of Rome's empire. If you wish to write about a specific war, such as Cesar's Gallic Campaign or the siege of Jerusalem, you will need to do specific research and these books are a good place to start.

* * *

After the fall of Rome, (476 CE) large permanent legions ceased to exist. The fighting man of the dark ages (such as a typical Viking oarsman) was a farmer or tradesman more often than a warrior. That being said—there were two groups of professional fighters who carried swords year round in the age of kings.

The noble class of the medieval era was strictly a warrior class. The man who lived in a castle did so by right of arms—meaning he would kill you if you tried to evict him. Sensibly, the sons of barons, dukes, and lords were trained from childhood to be killers.

By the time a young lord was sixteen or so, society expected him to be physically fit, mentally tough and skilled in all the arts of war. Knights needed to buy their own horses, weapons, and armor (the equivalent of buying your own jet fighter today). But, since they were from the ruling class they could easily afford the best.

Knights were the cream of the fighting crop and, mostly, they were loyal to the king who called on them as needed. Knights had "Sir" as a title added to their names, such as

Sir Lancelot. This practice carries over to our time when all military officers are now called "sir" (or ma'am as the case may be).

The other kind of medieval military professional was the man-at-arms. These were servants of a noble's house, paid to guard his family, and that's where their loyalty lied.

These soldiers guarded castles, caravans, city gates and so on. The men-at-arms trained (in their adult years, not since childhood) in the basics of fighting, and were fed slightly better than the peasants, so they were typically a bit stronger than average for the day. A man-at-arms had whatever weapons and armor his noble lord bought for him, and seldom would this include a horse.

When kings went to war with each other they would first have to "raise an army," as no standing one existed. Calling all loyal knights and ordering them to bring their men at arms raised such an army. However, when this was still not enough, more soldiers could be found by drafting the peasant "levies" (called levies because it was likened to a tax or toll the peasants must pay). Peasants, famously unskilled in war, would be given a crash course in fighting and sent into battle with some king's servant to lead them. These servants were often trusted veteran men-at-arms, and the word "servant" became "sergeant" over time.

In battle, men-at-arms would form "shield walls" and march at an enemy. A shield wall was a line of troops holding large shields that overlapped each other. Behind the shield wall would be troops with spears, halberds, and other long reach weapons. The front line's job was to advance on the enemy and stay alive while the men behind did most of the actual killing. This martial art is still practiced by a modern re-enactment group called the *Society for Creative Anachronism*, a group I was involved in for over ten years. It is an effective tactic but requires lots of practice to get a group of fighters to move as a team.

In modern grade school, many of us played some version of the game "steal the flag." In the middle ages, this was no game. Soldiers at that time wore no uniforms and had no way to distinguish friend from foe on a battlefield of several thousand men.

The solution was to follow your lord's flag. Each Baron and Duke would have a distinctive banner so their troops wouldn't get lost when following them into battle. Stealing the enemy's flag was a great way to sow confusion into your foe's ranks and break up a well-laid battle plan. Thus, soldiers would fight to the death to protect their flag, and this is part of the reason soldiers treat flags so reverently today.

A good read for any student of medieval warfare is William Shakespeare's *Henry V*. True, old Bill never fought in a war himself, but he lived in such a time and knew many soldiers. His play takes place during what many consider the height of the middle ages, the Hundred Years War between France and England. The play focuses on the King of England, of course, but it also details the plight of common English soldiers and even one Irish mercenary. Ironically, the battle that is won in the play, Agincourt, is one of the few historical examples where neither knights or men-at-arms carried the day—but archers.

ANCIENT & MEDIEVAL NAVIES

At times, the Romans maintained fleets of warships, but it was a sporadic history and can be seen as an exception to the historical trends of the ancient world, not the rule. Since ancient navies did not typically exist as permanent fleets, they were often called into existence during times of national emergency and disbanded soon afterward.

The occasional "permanent" fleets were made up of specially constructed warships with long rams in front positioned just under the water to punch holes in enemy ships. However, temporary navies would often be thrown together that contained merchant and fishing craft converted for the emergency. The sailors for these improvised navies were slaves, merchant seamen, and sometimes land soldiers who had no idea how to hoist a sail or steer a ship—nothing like on the job training.

Over time, it was found that the rams decreased a ship's maneuverability and in the late Middle Ages, they were discontinued altogether (Viking ships never had rams, to begin with). By the early Renaissance, advances in sail technology and cannons started to affect ship designs. However, throughout all these periods of change, the tactical goal was to board your enemy's ship with a large group of men and win victory at sword-point.

To learn more about the medieval naval ships of this later period, I recommend you go to http://www.maryrose.org for information on the Mary Rose. She was a ship of Henry the VIII's that sank in a storm in 1545. Bad luck for her crew no doubt, but fortunately for us, the wreck has been discovered and its archeology well documented. Its remains now grace a museum in Portsmouth, England.

The rule at sea during "peacetime" were pirates looking for victims, and everybody else just looking to get safely to port. It wasn't until the discovery of America that European powers started maintaining fleets of armed ships at all times and in all seasons.

When they did, they created military forces that more closely resembled pirate or merchant fleets than army units. In fact, a common practice was to grant a "letter of marquee" which allowed a pirate to legally prey on the enemy country's merchant shipping. This cost the king nothing, and it had the effect of doubling or even tripling his nation's naval power.

Though official navies became advantageous over time, the crews still resembled civilian seamen in many ways. For example, officers in European navies wore uniforms by the late 1600's (as referenced in Alexander Dumas' *The Three Musketeers*), but until the late 1800's common sailors did not. The exception was the captain's personal boat crew, who wore uniforms that the captain paid for himself.

A great movie about this period is *Master and Commander: the Far Side of The World*. It is well researched and based on a brilliant series of books, by Patrick O'Brien that are equally worth the reading.

CHAPTER II: THE US ARMY

Even if you do not intend to write about the modern army, I recommend you read this chapter. It covers a lot of general military principles here that are only referenced later for reasons of brevity.

***

Today, most armies of the world are professional fighting forces that exist year round. Flogging is gone, and soldiers are rarely executed. Modern warfare makes fighting shoulder-to-shoulder, in a literal fashion, a good way to commit suicide (one machine gun burst could effectively annihilate your entire group).

Still, soldiers do join for a contracted period of years like the Romans did and expect to receive benefits when they get out. In fact, a soldier can retire after twenty years and receive a pension just like the legionnaires did. Swords are no longer used in combat but still are worn with dress uniforms and seen on the unit insignia. In short, the modern army is the legacy of what was in the past and a hint of what it will be in the future.

THE ARMY TODAY

Pain! In my feet...Pain! In my legs...Pain! In my chest...
FEELS GOOD! I LIKE IT THERE!
- A modern running cadence song.

Becoming a soldier in modern times starts with a medical exam, a contract, and an oath. Next, the new soldier is sent to basic training, otherwise known as “boot camp” for about two months. Boot camp is a time of high stress and no personal freedom. The recruit is isolated from the rest of society and is “on the job” from sun up to sun down…and sometimes longer. Physical fitness training builds up strength and endurance while causing pain, cramps, and fatigue by the truckload. Marksmanship, wilderness survival, and first aid are some skills every army character should have. He or she will also learn how to march (yes, shoulder-to-shoulder) and the basics of military culture.

Nothing is considered too trivial to

drill into a recruit, from how to properly wear the uniform to how to fold underwear the military way. I recommend the movie *Full Metal Jacket* directed by Stanley Kubrick to get a feel of what recruit training is like. It concerns Marine training in the Viet-Nam era, but the other services have similar (although sometimes less intense) experiences for recruits.

Aside from military skills, boot camp teaches one other thing—honor. The military traditions of patriotism, courage, and selfless service are drilled into the recruit all the time. Are all soldiers honorable? No. "Dirt-bags" are soldiers who collect their pay and go through the motions of soldiering, but never develop that sense of "esprit de corps" (pride in one's group). These guys and gals are a drain on their unit…and sadly most units have at least one of 'em.

After boot camp, a soldier attends Advanced Individual Training. This is the school where he or she will learn an MOS (military occupational specialty). Any job you can think of in the civilian world probably has its military counterpart.

Remember, someone in the army needs to be a dental hygienist; otherwise, we lose troops to toothaches. Assuming every military character is some kind of ninja is a common fiction writer's fallacy that I personally find rather annoying.

ARMY RANKS

"Don't call me 'sir'! I WORK for a living!"

- Commonly heard sergeant's remark.

There are two basic types of rank in the army today and, as this structure started with the Romans; it will probably be around for a while. They are the officer ranks and the enlisted. Remember that Roman Centurion? That guy was an officer. Assuming he has a *list* of the one hundred legionnaires who answered to him, those would be his *enlist*ed men.

Get it? Good, because it's just that simple.

Like their ancient centurion ancestor or the medieval knight, the modern army officer is thought to be a nobler creature than those below them. The modern officer's parents do not buy their rank, but they probably did put them through college.

From the first day a soldier becomes an officer, troops are assigned for her to lead. A young lieutenant may only lead a platoon (about forty soldiers) to start with, but as she advances in rank, the numbers will grow until, as a general, the officer may lead the entire army.

Most officers start as officers. However, some do come up through the enlisted ranks. Enlisted soldiers who put themselves through college and then graduate from an officer-training program are rare but not unheard of. These former enlisted personnel are often called "mustangs."

All officer-training courses are harsh programs with very high standards. They are similar to boot camp but usually last a month longer and include the option to quit. That's right; a wannabe officer is allowed to quit officer training at any time. The quitter will never be an officer, however, because the military wants leaders who continue to try even when things are going badly.

There is one other way to become an officer. Sometimes, ancient kings would watch a brave man-at-arms in battle and make him a knight on the spot, and so it is today. A general can make any soldier an officer during combat. This is called earning a "battlefield commission," and it does not happen often. Any character thus promoted will surely be exceptional—or at least very lucky.

US Army officers start out as second lieutenants. If they survive long enough (and don't sleep with the general's daughter), they become captains within two or three years. After that, they can advance to major, and eventually, maybe, to lieutenant colonel.

None of these promotions are guaranteed, but they are reasonable expectations. Getting higher, however, is much harder. Few make it to full colonel, and general is an especially rare way to end a career. At this level of the officer ranks, political skill can mean as much as military proficiency and many good officers retire as majors or lieutenant colonels for this reason.

Officers are called "sir," or "ma'am," by everyone whom they outrank. For example, an enlisted man calls a captain "sir" and salutes him but so does a lieutenant.

Enlisted men are never saluted unless the room is very dark and the recruit is very new. (Or in the case of a soldier who has won the Congressional Medal of Honor—then even a General salutes that enlisted man…no, really). Enlisted personnel are required to salute officers when they get within a few yards. The only exception to this rule is during battle when saluting an officer is a good way to point out to an enemy sniper who is worth killing.

Officers do the planning for groups of soldiers, and they are the ones who think strategically on the battlefield. Strategy is a concept that covers everything from "do we attack at night or day," to "how do I make my enemy run out of supplies while conserving my own?"

U.S Amy currently divides officer ranks into the following order from lowest to highest:

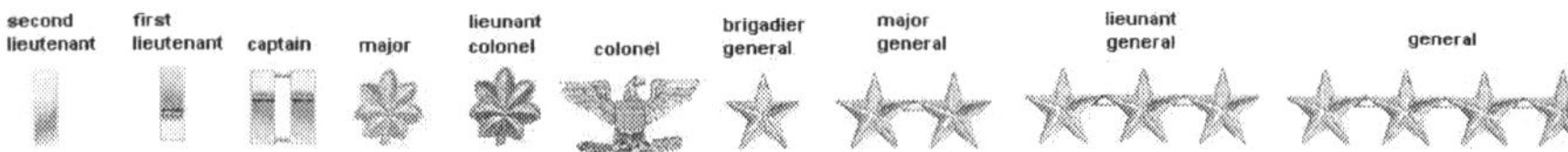

<u>Second Lieutenant</u>—*called a "butter bar" by enlisted men but not to his face.*

<u>First Lieutenant</u>—*sometimes called "LT" by enlisted men on friendly terms (pronounced "Ell Tee").*

Captain- *often the commander of a company.*

Major- *The lowest ranking "field grade" officer, and has the power to order a court-martial.*

Lieutenant Colonel—*sometimes called a "light colonel."*

Colonel- *Often called "the old man" but not to his face. They are also routinely referred to as a full-bird colonel.*

Brigadier General

Major General

Lieutenant General

General—*If God wore a uniform, it might be this one.*

Enlisted men need no college education and are often proud of their blue-collar roots. They attended the school of hard knocks and worked up through the ranks starting with private, then corporal and sergeant.

These soldiers do the "small picture" thinking in the army. Where the lieutenant plans the convoy across the desert, the private makes sure his gun-truck has gas and oil, the corporal makes sure everyone riding in that gun-truck carries a full load of ammo, and the sergeant makes sure every driver in that convoy's got a map and knows the lieutenant's plan.

The non-commissioned officers (NCOs) started their career at the bottom. They graduated from boot camp and spent a few years as privates before moving up, from corporals to sergeants. They are masters of tactics, the routines that dictate how troops fight in battle. NCOs have been in the army long enough to have made a few mistakes and learned from them.

A newly commissioned second lieutenant would be wise to listen to his platoon sergeant, but never to the point where the sergeant takes over the unit.

The US Army enlisted ranks go as follows:

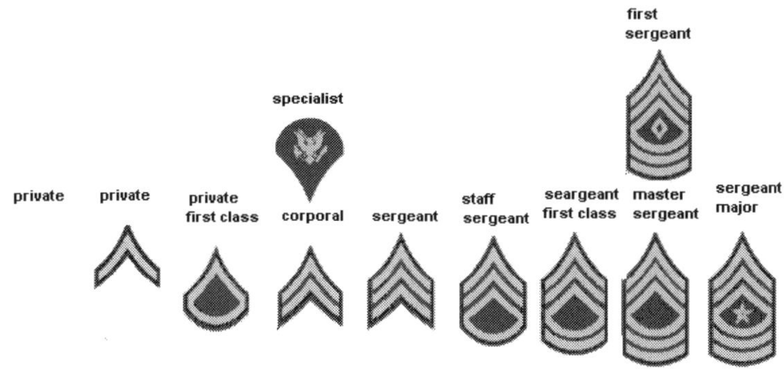

Private (Pv1)–*wear no rank insignia and never have.*

Private (Pv2)–*called "mosquito wings" for the single rank chevron.*

Private First Class—*has a "rocker" under the chevron.*

Corporal or Specialist—*the specialist rank has only been around since Viet-Nam. A specialist is paid the same as a corporal but has no NCO authority.*

Sergeant—*often called a "buck sergeant" for his youth.*

Staff Sergeant—*what I retired as.*

Sergeant First Class—*also called "platoon daddy."*

First Sergeant or Master Sergeant—*a first sergeant is called "top" as a sign of camaraderie & respect and is the senior enlisted person in a company. A master sergeant shares the same pay as top but is not the senior NCO in the company.*

Sergeant Major- *when God gets tired of kidding around, He wears this uniform*!

Rank matters; people don't always do what they are told, but for the soldier there are consequences. If a soldier disobeys an order from a superior, they can lose rank, pay, and possibly go to prison. Military prisons are not nice places and make civilian penitentiaries look like vacation spots.

Officers who are given orders they consider immoral can resign their commissions, which means they essentially quit their job. Enlisted personnel, however, are not allowed to quit and must serve until their contract is up.

The only time an enlisted soldier can disobey an order is when he believes it to be illegal (not simply immoral). A soldier cannot be ordered to rob a bank for instance or shoot a non-combatant. However, a soldier can be ordered to risk his life and if so must do it…no matter how suicidal the mission seems to be.

WARRANT OFFICERS

This third kind of rank, the warrant officer, has only been in the US Army since World War I. They are often called a "wobbly oh" as a nickname, but again, not to their face. Many units don't even have any warrant officers because they are only needed in very specialized roles. They are the technical experts, such as helicopter pilots, military intelligence agents, or master mechanics, and are not usually put in a leadership position, as that would distract them from their normal duties. These guys fall below the commissioned officer ranks but above enlisted soldiers.

Warrant officers are saluted, but one is not supposed to call them "sir." Instead, they are referred to as Mr. or Ms. When I served as a counterintelligence agent in Iraq; his team was supervised by a warrant officer.

ARMY LIFE IN GARRISON

"Garrison" refers to an army base. Garrison life consists of training sessions and paperwork to get ready for the next training session. Rules in garrison are strictly enforced, such as uniform standards and military protocol. The soldiers in garrison often work a forty-hour week, and afterward, go out to the movies or get in trouble with the local police.

Garrisons are also the places where weapons are stored, experimental technology is tested, valuable national secrets are hidden as in Area 51, and prisoners are incarcerated such as Fort Leavenworth.

ARMY LIFE IN THE FIELD

No combat-ready unit has ever passed inspection, and no inspection ready unit has ever survived combat.
- Murphy's Laws of Combat #1

"The field" refers to any remote place the army sends soldiers either for training or for war. Forget about the comfortable barracks; soldiers sleep on the ground. Showers are considered a luxury and the toilet (called a latrine) is wherever they dig with that small shovel the army gave them.

It's often said that some of the worst garrison soldiers are some of the best field soldiers. Experienced leaders know this and often relax rules in the field, especially during wartime.

ORGANIZATION OF ARMY UNITS

An army is organized into groups of soldiers called "units." NCOs lead small units, while larger units are led by an officer, called the "commander" (or CO). The commander usually has a fellow officer, one step below him in rank, who will serve as the "executive officer" (or XO). The XO handles most of the administrative tasks and is prepared to step up if the commander is killed.

There is always an NCO to guide the commander. This creates a leadership team with the commander always in charge but never alone.

The current US Army units are organized as follows:

Unit—Number of troops—Lead by a…

Fire Team—3 to 5—*corporal*

Squad—6 to10—*sergeant or staff sergeant*

Platoon—20 to 50—*sergeant first class and/or lieutenant*

Company—50 to 100—*captain with a first sergeant*

Battalion—350 to 500—*lieutenant colonel with a sergeant major*

Regiment—2,000 to 3,000 *colonel—with a sergeant major*

Brigade—3,000 to 6,000—*brigadier general with a sergeant major*

Division—10,000 to 20,000—*major general with a sergeant major*

Corps—20,000 to 40,000—*lieutenant general with a sergeant major*

Whole Damn Army—everybody—*Army Chief of Staff (a general) with the Sergeant Major of the Army*

As with our old Roman friends, US Army units are numbered, but they may also have nicknames. For instance, the 101st Airborne Division (which I served with) is known as "The Screaming Eagles," and the First Infantry Division is called "The Big Red One," and so on.

Units specialize in various roles on the battlefield, such as engineering, infantry or tanks. A battalion is usually made up of four companies, one of which is the headquarters company. The headquarters company has all the mechanics who keep the gun trucks rolling, the communications experts who keep the radio and satellite equipment talking (as I did on my first tour in Iraq), and the administrative staff who keep everybody paid and promoted. The headquarters company also might have a reconnaissance platoon or military intelligence squad who perform special missions in the field.

The other companies in a battalion are called "line companies" and are dedicated to the battalion's primary mission. For example—engineer battalions are devoted to military construction such as roads or forts.

An entire Division might be made of tank battalions (such as the 3rd Armored Division) or a corps devoted to aviation. Whatever the organization, soldiers in the US Army wear a patch on their left arm to signify what unit they are in. If they go to war with that unit, they may wear that same patch on their right arm for the rest of their service, no matter what other unit they later transfer to (a soldier who has never been to war is said to be "light on the right").

SPECIAL FORCES

There are several units in the US Army that can be rightfully considered elite. The 75th Ranger Regiment is one such example where members must attend the grueling Ranger School at Ft. Benning, Georgia for two months to qualify. However, I am devoting this section to the Special Forces because the "green berets" are often the writer's go-to-guys when they need an especially kick-ass character.

The Special Forces are a breed all to themselves. To earn the right to wear the green beret one must endure a grueling 62-week training program. The program is voluntary and one can quit at any time so only the extremely dedicated need apply. After training these guys Olympic athlete strong and have proven they are intelligent and cool-headed enough to be SF. Their primary mission is to sneak behind enemy lines and create an army of guerilla fighters from the local population. These soldiers not only need to know their job, they need to be able to teach it to the resistance fighters they recruit.

To recruit such an army, they are expected to be fluent in the local language and well acquainted with local's customs. As such they tend to be as much anthropologist as a soldier, able to quickly blend in with a foreign culture.

Beyond that, they are mortal—as military graveyards often attest. Their missions are typically so far into enemy territory no support from the rest of the army would get there in time if they needed rescue.

Also, there are said to be “Black OPs” for Special Forces, which are missions of an illegal nature—the kind where the president will deny you are part of the armed forces if you are caught. Naturally, this is el primo stuff for writing. You have small groups of elite characters doing exciting things in war zones. But do be careful not to mistake the Special Forces soldier with the regular guy who just wants to do his four-year tour and then split. These green berets are committed, and there are no “dirt-bags” in their ranks.

CONCLUSION

In the United States, the Army is America’s “senior service,” which means it is the oldest of our armed services. The army’s birthday is 14 June 1775 (Battle of Lexington and Concord), so it’s technically older than the nation it protects. It is also the largest service and has influenced all the other services in ways great and small.

For instance, the US Navy sent its pilots to train at the army's aviation school during World War II. The army issued brown shoes to everybody back then and navy fliers still wear brown shoes to this day.

Things like saluting; warrant officers, boot camp and making the lowest ranking guy clean the toilets are applicable to all the other services. What is different will be detailed in the next chapters.

CHAPTER III: THE NAVY AND MARINE CORPS

THE MODERN US NAVY

"...Whose arm hath bound the restless wave. Who biddest the mighty ocean deep. Its own appointed limits keep. Oh, hear us when we cry to Thee, for those in peril on the sea!"

US NAVY Hymn

The US Navy grew up quite separately from the US Army. In fact, as late as 1947, they were under separate parts of the government. The army was in the "War Department" while the navy was in the aptly named "Navy Department." Until the Department of Defense was created after World War II, the two services shared nothing of substance. The size and scale of the second world war illustrated the need for change and now all of the services work closely with one another (I once saw an air force general on a navy flagship in the middle east).

Since 1917, sailors have gone to boot camp just as soldiers do. Currently, all navy basic training takes place at Great Lakes Naval Training Center, near Chicago, Illinois (I attended it in the winter of 1987 and froze my butt off).

Just like in army basic training; patriotism, teamwork, and honor are drilled into the recruit. In addition, the sailor will learn knot tying, fire-fighting, damage control, and basic first aid, as well as gain a familiarity with rifles and pistols. The physical fitness training is not as intense in the navy as it is for the army or marines. The exception would be a sailor who is sent to an elite unit such as the Special Boat Teams or US Navy SEALS, in which case the physical training can be rather grueling.

Advanced training schools in the navy are called "A-schools," and many sailors spend several weeks learning electronics or some other skill after boot camp before actually going to sea. However, the navy will also send young sailors directly from basic training to the fleet, where they will "strike," which means to apprentice, for a rate. In the navy, a military occupational specialty is referred to as a "rate" and usually involves a job title and the word "mate," such as a machinist's mate, gunner's mate or electrician's mate.

The rates themselves are divided into three categories: firemen—work on the ship's engines, airmen—work on aircraft, and seamen—who do everything else. Thus, a sailor who is striking for the rate of Aviation Machinist's Mate but has yet to achieve that goal would be called an "airman apprentice."

Incidentally, every sailor in the US Navy has a chance to become part of the most elite scuba-commando unit in the world, the US Navy SEALs. About halfway through basic training, one of these super warriors will give a briefing to all the young sailors. The recruits are told what the SEALs are all about, and they are invited to take a special physical fitness test in a week's time. The test is not mandatory as the SEALS are only looking for volunteers. Few pass that test, but those who do are selected to go to Basic Underwater Demolition School

(BUDS) after they finish boot camp. BUDS is located in Coronado, California and the course runs for twenty-four weeks of living hell. Few pass BUDS and those who do are awarded the coveted SEAL trident pin to wear on their uniform so all will know that he's no ordinary sailor. In the end, from less than three percent of the sailors who take that special PT test in boot camp will ever wear that pin.

NAVY RANKS

The Navy's rank structure is divided into officer and enlisted ranks, just like the army. Navy officers are expected to be college graduates and must attend a rigorous twelve-week program called Officer Candidate School (OCS). Occasionally, an enlisted man is able to attend this course, but usually, a four-year degree is required.

A few of the navy's officers are graduates of the US Naval Academy in Annapolis, Maryland. It's a tough way to go to college, and the expression is; "No one sleeps at Annapolis except John Paul Jones."

By the way, Captain John Paul Jones is buried under the Annapolis chapel, and his body is guarded day and night by a Naval Honor Guard.

Annapolis offers an intense program and a great start. The contacts made at such an academy are extremely valuable to any officer's career and, like the army, the navy's highest ranks are filled with such graduates.

In the navy, the relationships between ranks are the same as with the army.

Officers are still called "sir," NCOs (called Petty Officers) still tend to the details of the missions, and the lowest ranks still scrub the toilets. Navy officers wear the same insignia on their working uniforms as army officers, and those symbols denote the same level of rank. On navy dress uniforms, officers have gold bands around their cuffs or on shoulder-boards to indicate rank.

What confuses most people, however, isn't the dress uniforms—it's the titles. For instance, an eagle on a collar indicates a "captain" in the navy, where that same symbol and authority is called a "colonel" in the army. If a navy officer is wearing two silver bars he's called a lieutenant, but he holds the same position of authority as an army captain. The navy does not apologize for this confusion! Instead, sailors just chuckle as soldiers fumble around looking lost on navy bases.

US Navy officer ranks are as follows:

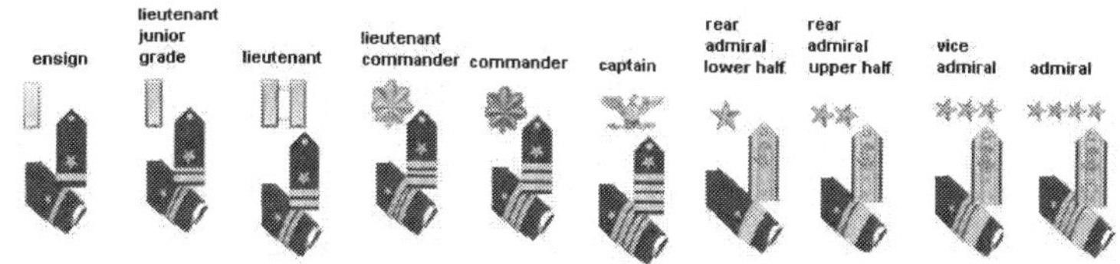

Ensign—*also called a" butter bar," but not to his face.*

Lieutenant Junior Grade—often called a "JG" for short.

Lieutenant—*equal to an army captain.*

Lieutenant Commander

Commander

Captain—*note the navy captain rank is the same as an army colonel.*

Rear Admiral Lower Half

Rear Admiral

Vice Admiral

Admiral

Now that sounds straightforward enough, but wait, this is the navy…there must be some bits of weirdness to confuse "land lubbers" (the non-seafaring folks of the world).

First, the term "captain" is not just a rank but also a title was given to any officer who is in charge of a ship. If you are on a small ship, the highest-ranking officer may only be a lieutenant commander. They would wear lieutenant commander's insignia and be paid like a lieutenant commander—but everybody would still call them "captain," go figure. It is also the case when a captain is killed in battle that the next ranking officer takes command and is suddenly addressed as "captain." On a famous ship of the navy of Peru, the Huáscar, this happened three times in the battle of Angamos as a lowly junior officer suddenly found himself captain of his nation's flagship.

Now the fact that "captain" is a title as well as a rank, naval tradition insists that there only be on person called captain on any ship. This can lead to some strange acrobatics when another person with the rank of captain sets foot on a ship. For instance, if an army captain comes aboard, he or she is referred to as "major." If another navy captain comes aboard, he or she is referred to as "commodore."

Now you're probably wondering what a "commodore" is.

A commodore is also a title, not a rank. It is used for an officer who leads a squadron of ships. Squadrons are anywhere between six to a dozen vessels that operate within a fleet as a subordinate unit. This officer may actually be a captain or an admiral, but he is still called "commodore"…fun!

I can draw an example of this tangle from my own time in the Persian Gulf. Back in 1988, I was assigned to Mine Countermeasures Group: a squadron of six old minesweeping ships sent to look for Iranian sea mines. Each minesweeping ship had a crew of only eighty sailors, and my "captain" was just a commander. The commodore of Mine Countermeasures Group held the rank of actual navy captain.

If you find this confusing, I invite you to use it as an opportunity for humor in your writing. Put your army captain who knows nothing of this on a ship and put all that confusion on him.

Navy enlisted ranks are as follows:

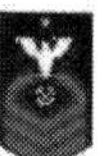

Seaman Recruit—*no rank insignia on working uniform. Only dress uniform has insignia.*

Seaman Apprentice—as above, no rank worn on working uniform.

Seaman—*female sailors are still called seaman. No rank on working uniform.*

Petty Officer Third Class—*my highest navy rank. Rank worn on all uniforms.*

Petty Officer Second Class

Petty Officer First Class

Chief Petty Officer—*Called "chief" or chief boats if a boatswain's mate.*

Senior Chief Petty Officer—*has one star on top of his rank insignia.*

Master Chief Petty Officer—*has two stars on top, usually only one of these per ship.*

The navy also has warrant officers for

technical specialties like the army does. They are not able to serve as pilots, however, as only the army allows warrants to fly aircraft.

Petty officers and above are NCOs and have a tradition of leadership similar to the army's sergeants. But, because this is the navy, we have to change things around to mess with the land lubber's heads even more.

A petty officer is seldom called a petty officer. Instead, he is referred to by his rate. Thus, a petty officer second class, who is also a gunner's mate, will be addressed as "gunners mate second class." Sometimes sailors even abbreviate that, when talking about a second class electrician's mate they might just call him EM2 Smith. Confused yet? Yep, it's the navy, what ya' going to do?

NAVY AT SEA

Imagine you wake up at work. All your co-workers are right there with you. You all have breakfast together, go do your jobs, and at night as you watch the sun sink low…you're still at work. Welcome to life at sea. Today, like hundreds of years ago and as it will probably be hundreds of years from now, sailors spend most of their time at sea. This is where the job gets done and is occasionally where the action takes place.

Life at sea can go from mind-numbingly dull to life and death very quickly. On routine days, sailors do maintenance work on the ship, cook meals, and stand watches, and conduct drills to keep in shape for combat. On not so routine days, sailors battle storms, rescue stranded people in the middle of the ocean, fight the enemy, and pray they will reach shore safely.

NAVY IN PORT

Port is where a ship comes in to rest, refit, re-supply, and repair. It is usually a town or city with a deep-water shore for ships to maneuver in, and either civilian or military docks. If it's a "home-port," the family of the crew lives in this place and it will be an actual navy base. In short, life for the sailor in homeport is a lot like the soldier's life in garrison.

Foreign ports are another matter altogether. A foreign port is a place unfamiliar to most of the crew and far away from home. The people have strange customs, and most sailors can't speak the local language. The layout of the city is unknown, but the beer is a lot cheaper than in the USA!

After weeks to months cooped up on a ship, with nothing to spend your money on, three days in Singapore can be quite an adventure (I still have the tattoo).

In foreign ports, the navy always forms a "shore patrol." This is a group of petty officers, drawn from the ship's crew to look for drunken sailors who are about to run afoul of the local police. They wear dress uniforms and black armbands with the letters SP. Typically, the shore patrols are only armed with billy-clubs. A sailor may fight or run from the shore patrol, but getting nabbed by them is always preferred to experiencing the hospitality of a foreign jail.

TYPES OF SHIPS

This covers a wide selection from aircraft carriers to small patrol vessels. The US Navy also has specialized vessels like hospital ships, freighters, and mine sweepers. If the ship's captain is only a lieutenant commander, you are on a very small ship (a "small boy" is the term) with fewer than one hundred sailors. Aircraft carriers are at the opposite end of the spectrum and have several officers of the rank of captain (but only one in charge of the entire ship) to manage thousands of seamen.

In general, navy vessels fall into one of these categories:

<u>Captain's Gig</u>—*this is the personal boat of the captain. It can be any type of boat on the ship that he chooses to use and may also be used for mundane tasks as well.*

<u>Admiral's Badge</u>—*this is the personal boat of the fleet's admiral. It is the only boat in the fleet painted black.*

<u>Patrol Boat</u>—*heavily armed boat used for river patrol, as in the movie Apocalypse*

Now.

Corvette—*fast attack ship for reconnaissance and raiding.*

Frigate—*beefed up corvette capable of landing helicopters on its deck.*

Destroyer—*nicknamed "tin can," made to sink enemy small ships and subs.*

Freighter—*keeps the fleet re-supplied at sea so they can stay in the fight longer.*

Cruiser—*more heavily armed than a destroyer but same mission.*

Submarine—*in modern times these come in two varieties; "fast attack" subs seek out and kill other vessels, and "boomers" can carry nuclear weapons that can kill civilization.*

Battleships—*huge cannons pack a very hard punch, but they are slow and make big fat targets. No new battleships have been built since World War II. (Sometimes called a battlewagon)*

Aircraft Carriers—*often a whole fleet will be centered on supporting a 'carrier. These big boys are sent around the world to say the*

US means business! Such is their value, that smaller ships are ordered to ram enemy torpedoes (which will sink a small ship easily) to prevent damage to a 'carrier.

Flagship—*any ship in a fleet chosen by the admiral to be the center of his command. Because admirals have large staffs of officers under them, this ship is usually the largest in the fleet to accommodate the extra people.*

ORGANIZATION OF SHIP'S DIVISIONS

Ships are organized into divisions of varying sizes, depending on the size of the ship. An aircraft carrier has about 3,000 sailors and will have about a hundred and twenty divisions, whereas my little minesweeper had only eighty sailors and maybe five divisions. Whether fifty or five; the idea is to group sailors of similar skills to perform duties required on the ship.

Examples are: the Engineering Division, which keeps the ship's engines going, or the Operations Division which mans the radar and steers the ship, Deck

Division handles shipboard maintenance and so on.

The classic TV show, *Star Trek,* differentiated the Starship Enterprise's divisions by having the crew wear different colored shirts (blue for science, gold for command, red for engineering—and so on). If your characters are part of a space navy, they will probably be similarly put into divisions such as the Computer and Sensors Division, or maybe the Laser and Missile Battery Division. Colored shirts are optional of course.

DAMAGE CONTROL

Don't give up the ship!

- Last words of Captain James Lawrence, War of 1812

Damage control is a critical part of naval combat. The enemy is trying to sink your ship, and you are trying to stop them. While the gunner's mates are loading shells into the cannons, everybody else isn't just whistling Dixie.

The entire crew is trained in damage

control, and is expected to do everything possible to save the ship first and their shipmates second. That's right; sailors are told to ignore the screams of the wounded until the ship is no longer leaking or burning, then tend to the injured.

Divisions are organized into "damage control teams." Each team is lead by a chief or first class petty officer. They have all the tools and training needed to put out a fire, stop flooding, pump seawater overboard, and evacuate causalities. They keep the ship floating and fighting no matter what!

THE MODERN US MARINES

"The marines are a department of the navy...

The men's department!"

- Spoken by almost any (male) marine with a beer or two in him.

The army has many corps which refers to groups of soldiers larger than a division. The US Marine Corps (nicknamed the "jarheads") is, in fact, a corps of the US

Navy. That being said, marines have their own unique uniforms and traditions. Sailors do not go to marine boot camp, and marines do not go to navy boot camp. However, marine officer cadets do go to the US Navy Academy at Annapolis with classmates who will one-day command submarines and aircraft carriers.

Yep, things are weird in navy land.

Simply put, the US Marines are elite troops that ride on ships so they can be quickly sent to any trouble spot in the world with a seacoast. In the early twentieth century, they were known as the "State Department boys," because they often were the only force available to support US policy in foreign lands (in fact they WERE the government of Haiti from 1915 to 1934). On land, they work closely with any US or allied army units they encounter to defeat the enemy and secure US interests overseas.

The marines rely on the navy for a lot of support. The Navy Medical Corps, for example, provides the marines with 100% of its medical personnel. When wounded marines call out for a "corpsman," they are asking for some sailor with an aid bag to save their lives…and that sailor will come! They also rely on the Navy Chaplin Corps and Judge Advocate General Corps, which are both mixtures of navy and marine personnel.

In science fiction, the soldiers of space are almost exclusively called "marines." The idea of space marines probably originated with the notion such troops would have to be transported in ships, and on crowded space ships, there would only be room for the best troops.

If we do ever have space marines, I envision them as experts in zero gravity warfare. Such troops would be boarding enemy spacecraft in armored vacuum-sealed space suits. They would be adept at hand to hand and close quarter battle and be just the troops you want to take over an enemy space station. On a planet, however, you would prefer troops with expertise in that specific planet's environment, with lots of tanks and other heavy equipment that could not fit in just any spaceship. Thus, in this future, the marines would rule the stars, and the army would get the dirt.

THE MAKING OF A MARINE

Becoming a marine involves twelve weeks of boot camp (the longest basic training of any of the services). The US Marine Corps has only two places used for basic training, Paris Island on the east coast and San Diego on the west. Incidentally, San Diego graduates are called "Hollywood Marines." Physical fitness, marksmanship, wilderness survival, and first aid are taught, as well as how to march (yes, shoulder-to-shoulder), and the basics of military culture. As stated earlier, I recommend the movie *Full Metal Jacket* directed by Stanley Kubrick to get a feel of what recruit training is like.

The marines are especially known for instilling a sense of "esprit de corps" in their recruits. The saying goes, "Once a marine, always a marine," and once discharged they refer to themselves as "former-marines," never "ex-marines."

After boot camp, marines attend Advanced Individual Training just like a soldier would, except they do not choose which school they will attend—it's chosen for them. The marines are not just made up of infantry grunts but have tank crews, artillery batteries, and computer technicians too (many of which train at army schools).

MARINE RANKS

The US Marines divide its troops into enlisted and officer ranks and has a lot in common with the US army's rank titles. However, "similar" does not mean the same, and there are differences.

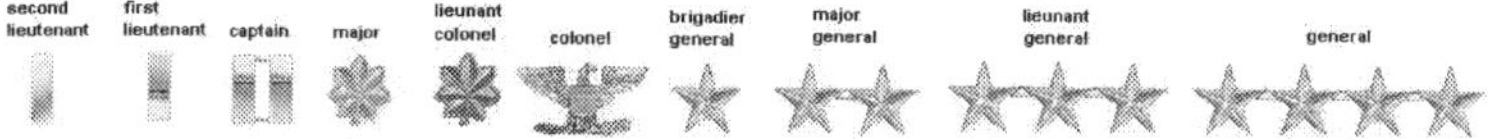

Second Lieutenant—*called a "butter bar" by enlisted men, but not to his face.*

First Lieutenant—*sometimes called "LT" by enlisted men on friendly terms.*

Captain

Major

Lieutenant Colonel—*sometimes called a "light colonel."*

Colonel—*often called "the old man" but not*

to his face. They are also routinely referred to as a full bird or full bird Colonel.

<u>Major General</u>

<u>Lieutenant General</u>

<u>General</u>—*the highest ranking marine general is called "the Commandant" no other service uses this title for its most senior officer.*

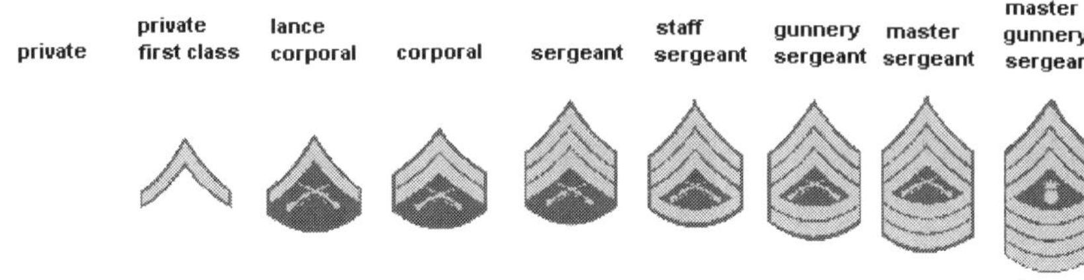

Private (Pv1)—wear no rank insignia and never have.

Private (Pv2)—called "mosquito wings" for the single rank chevron.

Lance Corporal—have a crossed rifles under the single chevron.

Corporal

Sergeant—often called a "buck sergeant" for his youth.

Staff Sergeant

Gunnery Sergeant—also called "gunny."

Master Gunnery Sergeant—sometimes called "first sergeant" if they are the top NCO in a company.

Sergeant Major—when God gets tired of kidding around, He wears this uniform!

The marines also have warrant officers who are addressed as "mister" or "missus" and serve as technical specialists in fields like supply and maintenance, but never as aircraft pilots. Like the navy, only commissioned officers fly aircraft in the marines.

ORGANIZATION

The marines are organized into fireteams, squads, platoons and such—just like the US Army. However, they do not wear patches on their sleeves designating their unit. Instead, every marine has the eagle, globe, and anchor emblem stitched over their left shirt pocket.

The marines are also often organized into Marine Expeditionary Units (MEUs) built around a re-enforced infantry battalion, and sent to sea with the navy. There, they try to train on the cramped navy ships, while waiting for the possibility they will be sent ashore.

If they go to shore in a foreign port of call, they will have experience exactly like the sailors (even running from the same shore patrol). If they go to shore for war, they neutralize any threat to American interests. The navy will support the jar-heads with air strikes from the carriers and bombardment from the battleships, but the marines are the ones who go in for the close kill.

CONCLUSION

There is an intense rivalry between the US Navy and the Marine Corps. The marine will call a sailor a "squid" as a derogatory term, and a sailor will reply that "a squid is a superior form of marine life." The only time these two services aren't trying to get each other's goat is during the annual Army/Navy football game when marines cheer as hard as the sailors to see the army beaten. It has always been, and always will be, a love-hate relationship.

CHAPTER IV: THE AIR FORCE

The army, navy, and marines date back to the time of the American Revolution. The air force (nicknamed "the zoomies") was founded just after World War II. Before that, they were called the US Army Air Corps and their origins date back to the dawn of flight when army balloons were used in the Civil War to locate the enemy. Air force basic training is similar to the navy's, in that it is more about technical skills than physical fitness. As in all basic training programs, honor, and discipline are major parts of the curriculum and need not be repeated here. Airmen also go to advanced training to learn an AFSC (Air Force Specialty Code) which is the Air Force's term for an MOS—similar to the Marine Corps and army's job system.

All US military services use aircraft and have pilots. The navy and its marines specialize in small aircraft which can be launched from a ship. The US Army uses lots of helicopters for moving troops and supplies on the battlefield (which is why army warrant officers fly, the army has the greatest need for pilots). The US Air Force specializes in large fixed-wing aircraft, such as cargo planes and bombers. So when the US Army wants to attack the enemy with paratroopers from the sky, they need to ask the US Air Force for a lift.

Smaller air force planes, such as fighters, support the bigger ones in combat. The air force also maintains the inter-continental ballistic missiles that were developed to nuke the Soviet Union during the Cold War. If you want to aim even higher, there is the Space Command where the USAF maintains and operates our military satellites.

In science fiction, the navy usually commands space forces, but the air force is already doing that today. Although there is no space military fleet, there may one day be. The old structures of the wet water navy may not adapt to the new frontier, and perhaps the commander of your starship should be addressed as colonel.

If you want to see a good air force movie, I recommend *Dr. Strangelove,* starring Peter Sellers. *Dr. Strangelove* is a dark comedy about World War III made in the 1960s. Aside from being a masterwork of film, *Dr. Strangelove* shows how the air force thinks about, and may one day fight, global thermonuclear war. You'll find yourself rooting for the bomber crew that is about to unknowingly end the world, but it's still a good movie.

AIR FORCE RANKS

The air force has the same officer ranks as the army and a totally different set of enlisted ranks designed to annoy the crap out of every other service. An army private is an air force "airman." The air force has no corporals or specialists, so the title of staff sergeant is given at one-step lower—thus, an army corporal and air force senior airman are equals. Weird, I know.

<u>Second Lieutenant</u>—*called a "butter bar" by enlisted men, but not to his face*

<u>First Lieutenant</u>—*sometimes called "LT" by*

enlisted men on friendly terms

Captain

Major

Lieutenant Colonel—*sometimes called a "light colonel"*

Colonel—*often called "the old man" but not to his face. They are also routinely referred to as a full bird or full bird colonel.*

Brigadier General

Major General

Lieutenant General

General

Airman Basic—wear no rank insignia, and yes, women are also called "airmen."

Airman—single rank chevron

Airman First Class—two chevrons

Senior Airman—three chevrons. Sometimes

called a sergeant

Staff Sergeant—four chevrons

Tech Sergeant—five chevrons

Master Sergeant—called a "first sergeant" if they are the senior sergeant in a unit

Senior Master Sergeant

Chief Master Sergeant

The interesting thing about the air force officer/enlisted relationship is that the officers insist on being the guys in the planes. In the early days of World War I, when the zoomies were part of the army, sergeants were allowed to fly fighters in combat…but no more.

This has led to a situation where the majority of air force enlisted men sit back at the base and drink beer every night, while "sir" is getting shot at flying over someplace dangerous. This may explain why a certain zoomie colonel and major go through the "stargate" in a weekly TV show of the early 2000s to visit other planets while sergeants are left behind to "encode chevrons."

The air force does have some enlisted

elite warriors. However, they just don't have a very cool name…they are called the "PJs."

AIR FORCE SPECIAL FORCES

The "para-jumpers" (or PJs for short) are commandos with a very specific mission: bring the pilot home. Pilots get shot down over every known environment on Earth. They crash in mountains, deserts, oceans, and over polar ice. They crash during peacetime and in wartime and enemy soldiers may be hunting them on the ground.

When the pilot's parachute brings him to ground, he may already be injured and need medical help…and help is on the way. The PJs are trained to go anywhere on a moment's notice to get that pilot home if it can possibly be done. They are expert medics and wilderness survivalists. Highly skilled in combat, they are bad enough that you really don't want to get in their way as they rescue the downed zoomie.

AIR FORCE UNITS

The smallest unit is a "flight," consisting of three to four planes led by a captain. Next in size is a "squadron," consisting of four to five flights led by a lieutenant colonel. The air force "wing" is made up of twelve to fifteen squadrons led by a general. All of these units have maintenance crews of enlisted personnel to service the aircraft. Pilots are expected to be experts on navigating and fighting with their planes, while enlisted personnel load the missiles, repair battle damage and pump the fuel.

Of course, the air force doesn't just consist of flying units. They have units that run hospitals or provide base security as well. An airman (the term for all USAF personnel in general) will wear his unit patch over his left shirt pocket. Unlike the army, the air force has no tradition of "combat patches." Otherwise, air force units are similar to the armies because of the air force's common heritage with the army.

PRISONERS OF WAR

Because air force pilots are often over enemy territory when they get shot down, many of them end up as missing-in-action or prisoners of war (POWs).

True, the PJs will try to rescue them, and any army, navy or marine forces nearby will also run to their aid…if possible. The fact remains however that, historically, enemy POW camps have more US pilots than are represented in the services in general. For this reason, all pilots are trained in survival, escape, and evasion tactics. It is hoped this training will help them evade the enemy long enough to get rescued.

In World War II, there was a special unit of American adventurers flying for the Chinese Nationalist military (long story). Known as the "Flying Tigers," these guys even went so far as to sew a silk sign on the back of their jackets to help them if shot down. Since they flew over China, they had the signs written in Chinese. It was called a "blood chit, " and it essentially read, "I am an American. Help me and you will be rewarded." The intention was for a downed pilot to be able to ask for help from the local people as he evaded the Japanese Army.

If all else fails, and a serviceman is caught, there is a specific code to follow while in captivity. The Code of Conduct was instituted after the Korean War as a guide for ethical conduct while imprisoned. All US military personnel are taught this code and expected to live by it while in captivity.

Article I: I am an American, fighting in the armed forces which guard my country and our way of life. I am prepared to give my life in their defense.

Article II: I will never surrender of my own free will. If in command, I will never surrender the members of my command while they still have the means to resist.

Article III: If I am captured, I will continue to resist by all means available. I will make every effort to escape and to aid others in escape. I will accept neither parole or special favors from the enemy.

Article IV: If I become a POW, I will keep faith with my fellow prisoners. I will give no information or take part in any action that may be harmful to my comrades. If I am senior, I will take command, if not I will obey the lawful orders of those above me and back them up in every way.

Article V: If questioned, I am required to give name, date of birth and service number. I will evade answering further questions to the best of my ability. I will make no oral or written statements disloyal to my country or its allies.

Article VI: I will never forget that I am an American, responsible for my actions, and dedicated to the principals that made my country free. I will trust in my God and the United States of America.

CONCLUSION

Of all the services, the air force is considered the "softest." They are often derided as the "chair force" for their numerous desk jobs. They have much lower physical fitness standards than the army or marines and their barracks and recreational facilities are often the most comfortable of all. A military urban legend goes like this: the army opens a base by building the training facilities, and maintenance shops, then they ask Congress for more funds to build housing and recreation facilities…the air force builds housing, theaters, pools, and golf courses, then asks congress for the funds to build the runway.

The air force is also known for a more relaxed attitude regarding officer-enlisted relationships. Depending on circumstances and duty assignment, there is generally less attention to military protocol amongst the zoomies. With all that said, the air force kicks a lot of ass for the USA.

Air power is often the most decisive factor in victory on the battlefield today. An army expression is, “When all else fails…call in an air strike.” Keep in mind; it was largely due to the US Air Force’s thirty-seven-day bombardment that compelled the Iraqi Army to surrender to US forces in the First Gulf War. Many US “interventions” do not even involve ground troops anymore, such as the Kosovo Campaign of 1999, or Libya in 2011. With the growing role of drone aircraft and satellites in modern war, the chair force just may be the new tip of American’s sword.

CHAPTER V: THE COAST GUARD

Everyone who joins the Coast Guard has to be at least six feet tall. That way if their ship sinks they can walk to shore.

- A very old Navy joke

The Coast Guard is part of the US military…No, it's not!…Yes, it is! Okay, so it sometimes is and sometimes isn't.

The US Coast Guard was founded when two other federal, non-military services, combined in 1915. The "US Revenue Marine," which was charged with catching smugglers trying to avoid import tax, and the "US Life Saving Service," which maintained lighthouses and had teams of sailors ready to row out into a storm to rescue seamen at a moment's notice. Their first wartime role during World War I was to look for German U-Boats in the Atlantic.

The "coasties" still patrol our coastline looking for criminals, and rescuing seamen from storms and accidents at sea. The movie *The Guardian,* starring Kevin Kostner, is about such guys and it's a pretty good flick.

I also recommend *The Finest Hour,* starring Craig Gillespi, which portrays a daring rescue set in the 1950s.

But the role of the coast guard is ever expanding. Coast guard personnel were doing a port security mission in Basra during the Iraq War, and I met a few who were working north of Baghdad; leading to the question; "What coast are they guarding anyway?"

When the nation is at war, the coast guard legally becomes part of the US Navy and is used accordingly. In fact, the only coast guard Medal of Honor recipient, so far, was killed while saving US Marines. Petty Officer Douglas Munro put his boat in front of a Japanese machine gun during World War II so some trapped jar-heads could escape. He died, the marines lived, and the medal was presented posthumously to his family.

The coast guard uses all of the navy ranks, and their basic recruit training and apprentice training are similar to the navy as well. However, there are some important departures.

An interesting thing about the regular

US services is that by law the military can't arrest US civilians…but as a civilian agency the coast guard can. All coastguardsmen who hold the rank of petty officer, or above, are sworn federal law enforcement agents with powers of arrest.

The coast guard is historically short on funds so they stretch their resources any way they can. I once spent two weeks in the Caribbean on the navy ship USS Blakely, looking for drug smugglers. When the Blakely found a suspected vessel, a team of coast guard sailors was sent to board her and make arrests if they found anything. The twelve "coasties" didn't like the navy food much but loved Jamaica and were thrilled to finally get to visit a foreign port.

COAST GUARD RANKS

The US Coast Guard uses the exact same rank structure as the US Navy in every respect.

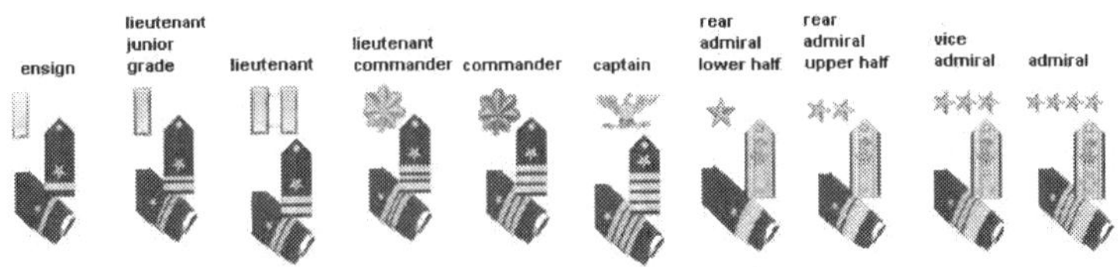

Ensign—*also called a" butter bar" but not to his face.*

Lieutenant Junior Grade

Lieutenant—*equal to an army captain.*

Lieutenant Commander

Commander

Captain—*note the coast guard captain rank is the same as an army colonel.*

Rear Admiral Lower Half

Rear Admiral

Vice Admiral

Admiral

Seaman Recruit—wears no rank insignia.

Seaman Apprentice—wear two slash marks.

Seaman—Yes female sailors are still called seaman-wear three slash marks.

Petty Officer Third Class—eagle with one chevron.

Petty Officer Second Class—eagle with two chevrons.

Chief Petty Officer—called "chief" to his face a 'rocker' connects the eagle to his three chevrons.

Senior Chief Petty Officer—has two stars on top of his rank insignia.

Master Chief Petty Officer—has two stars on top, usually only one of these guys per ship.

CONCLUSION

The coast guard is hard to pigeonhole, and the government has even had problems deciding where they belong. Once part of the Treasury Department, they were moved to the Department of Transportation in 1967, and now are part of the Department of Homeland Security. That is unless there is a declared war and then they become part of the Department of Defense under the navy as mentioned above. Coast guardsmen tend to operate from small, isolated bases and have little contact with the other services. They also have a lot more official interaction with civilians than the other services due to their law enforcement and maritime safety roles.

Because of their small size, the coasties can be very picky about who they recruit. They have high standards and, in their own way, are every bit as elite as the US Marines.

Writers who wish to focus on the US Coast Guard should know they are in good company. Alex Haley, the author of *Roots*, was a coast guard sailor and the founder of their military journalism rate.

CHAPTER VI: TACTICS

LAND TACTICS

"As to tactics, I always felt it was best to get there the first with the most men."

- General N.B. Forrest Confederate Army

There are many books written on this subject—thick ones. It is not the goal of this book to describe the entire subject; however, a general understanding is helpful to the writer who wants to get off to a good start.

The word "tactics" is used to describe how one fights. For instance, in the American Revolution, the standard musket was very inaccurate and had a rather short range. To maximize the killing potential of these clumsy weapons, armies fired in volleys (ready, aim, fire). Troops of that age were trained to quickly fire a few short-range volleys and then charge the enemy with steel bayonets. And as tactics go, this worked well for the time.

Of course, we don't fight like that anymore. Advances in weapons' technology force new tactics to be developed, and the process is ongoing…which is why you have a lot of thick books out there.

Modern armies have naturally adapted to these new weapons and come up with some effective tactics. Machine guns and explosives have made it just plain suicide to cluster in a large group (big target) or in open country (easy target). Whenever possible, the modern soldier wants to be in “cover and concealment,” and tactics are used to facilitate that. Cover, by the way, is anything that stops bullets, such as brick walls or the dirt of a foxhole. Concealment is anything that makes a soldier hard to see such as darkness, tree branches, and tall grass.

BOUNDING OVERWATCH

Despite what you may see in action movies, it’s not possible for most folks to aim a weapon while running full speed, so soldiers don’t try to. When soldiers have to move fast through the open ground (no cover or concealment) they use a tactic called “bounding over-watch.”

This means half of the soldiers available will run as fast as they can across the open ground and then dive for cover (known as a 3 to 5-second rush). As the training mantra goes, "I'm up, he sees me, I'm down."

The other half will stay in cover and shoot the hell out of any enemy they see. Then, the second half will run across that same open ground while the first half shoots enemies for them and so on. Typically, this is how a squad moves, one fire team at a time, across open ground when they expect the enemy to be present.

HOW TO AMBUSH

"No sorry son-of-a-bitch ever won a war by dying for his country. He won it, by making the OTHER sorry son-of-a-bitch die for HIS country!"

-General Gorge S. Patton

The magic letter is "L." By this, it's

meant that the ideal setup is to create a letter "L," as seen from above, by having one unit from the vertical part of the letter, and another equal sized unit from the horizontal. Typically, these will be squad-sized units of about ten troops apiece. Where is the enemy? Why the enemy is caught in a vicious crossfire between two units of soldiers blasting away at 'em from two sides.

When soldiers set up an ambush, they try to find a spot they know the enemy will be moving through and then form that "L" of hidden soldiers around the spot. This spot becomes known as the "kill zone." When the enemy enters the kill zone, both squads start shooting at the same time and aren't in any danger of hitting their friends as only the enemy is in sight (One can see why the letter L was chosen over an O without too much thought on the matter).

Thus, the enemy is trapped under a vicious hail of gunfire from two directions before he gets a chance to fight back. The goal is the total destruction of all enemy troops in the kill zone. It is not the intent of an ambush to take prisoners.

No, this is not a fair fight. Professionals don't fight fair. Don't be in a kill zone, stay out of an enemy's "L!"

ROOM CLEARING

When American soldiers enter a building today, they move fast to "L out" the room. Within seconds, a door is busted open, and two of the room's four walls are suddenly lined with soldiers. In Iraq, this was a common way to enter a house if insurgents were suspected within. As houses also tend to have families inside soldiers had to use discretion. Anyone who offers resistance is shot, and once the room is secured, soldiers move into the next one and go through the house in this manner.

Sadly, insurgents often hide among the civilian population. The phenomena known as COBs (Civilians On Battlefield) is an old and often tragic story. A good writer would do well to keep this in mind when writing of the "glory" of war…enough said.

RECOMMENDED READING

For further study of basic modern army tactics, there is no better book than E.D. Swinton's *The Defense of Duffer's Drift*. Swinton was a general in the British Army and the founder of Britain's tank corps. His book is informative, enlightening, short and, surprisingly, fun to read.

The book is set in the South African Boer War of 1900. This war was fought between the British Empire and Dutch guerrilla farmers known as the Boers. It was a modern war in the sense that it was fought with high-powered rifles and machine guns. It was also the first time the term "commando raid" was used ("Commando" was the Boer word for "militia unit").

In his book, Swinton describes a series of dreams a young officer has about a battle. Each dream describes the exact same battle over and over again. But, in each dream the officer makes different decisions and gets different results, beginning with disaster and ending with victory. It is only a seventy-two-page book and is required reading at many US Army schools.

SEA TACTICS

Surrender? I have not yet begun to fight!

- Captain John Paul Jones, American Revolution

The American naval Captain, John Paul Jones (who now sleeps at Annapolis), made the above quote as his ship was both burning and sinking.

As the Royal naval captain of the HMS Serapis watched the American's plight, the Brit invited the American to surrender, but it proved to be a waste of breath.

Not only did Captain Jones refuse to surrender, but he also put his surviving men in rowboats, climbed aboard the Serapis with pistols and swords to defeat the British. As the Americans watched their former ship sink, they hauled down the Union Jack and hoisted up the Stars and Stripes over the US Navy's newest warship. Thus bears out the military maxim for land and sea; "never quit."

Another important rule of warfare to remember is; "surprise is a good thing when it's on your side." In World War I, German submarines were the rulers of the Atlantic. Without warning, U-Boats would strike and devastate allied shipping. The Allies tried hunting for subs, but finding them was next to impossible because sonar wasn't available until the last years of the war and then only in prototype form.

British officers, however, soon learned the sup captain's tactics. The Germans would fire torpedoes at large merchant ships while underwater, but they would attack smaller craft quite differently. Because torpedoes were expensive, a German captain would bring his U-Boat to the surface to sink smaller merchant ships using a cannon mounted on the sub's deck. So, the Royal Navy developed the Q-Ship as a response. A Q-Ship looked like a small unarmed merchant ship, but when a U-Boat surfaced the British sailors knocked down fake walls to reveal they had cannons of their own.

It worked pretty well.

However, another naval rule that will always apply, no matter what technology dominates, is to fight in groups. A lone ship is vulnerable to attack by a group of ships. Once the Germans lost submarine UB-68 to the allies, its captain, Von Donitz, had a lot of time to think while relaxing in a prisoner of war camp.

He conceived of the "wolf pack" to solve the Q-ship problem. He envisioned a group of three to five submarines working together so if a Q-Ship revealed itself it could be easily torpedoed by a U-Boat that remained underwater. Unfortunately, for the Germans, the "wolf pack" idea had to wait until Von Donitz got out of prison. He later became a German admiral in World War II and was famous for surrendering his nation to the Allies after Hitler's suicide.

Remember, every move has a countermove. A good captain stays as many moves ahead of his enemy as he can. I highly recommend the movie *Master and Commander: The Far Side of The World* starring Russell Crowe for an understanding of sailing ship tactics and sea life in general. Not only is it one of the best movies ever made, but it also shows how surprise and deception are critical factors in victory at sea. If you want ideas for space navy tactics, I can recommend *The Lost*

Fleet series by Jack Campbell. Mr. Campbell goes out of his way to explain how space navies fight in his universe, even taking into account the effects of relativity as one approaches light speed, and it is sure to give the science fiction tactician some ideas.

AIR TACTICS

The invention of the airplane changed war, unlike anything since man first learned to ride a horse. The battlefield is now three dimensional, and no one can ignore the threat from the sky. Of course, technology is always changing, but the fundamental physics of flight have not. Planes still need room to turn and maneuver, and fuel must be burned to maintain altitude and speed.

An early German ace, Oswald Boelcke, (no, not the Red Barron) developed a list of rules for winning dogfights called "The Dicta Boelcke." The Dicta was taught to many of Germany's top fighter pilots in World War I, and many of these rules still apply today.

THE DICTA BOELCHE:

1. Try to secure the upper hand before attacking. If possible, keep the sun behind you (in the age of heat-seeking missiles, this is still very good advice).

2. Always continue with an attack you have begun.

3. Open fire only at close range, and only when you have your opponent squarely in your sights (In the age of long-range missiles this is not necessarily the thing to do, but if all you have is machine guns with limited ammunition, it applies).

4. Keep your eye on your opponent and don't be deceived by ruses.

5. Assail your opponent from behind.

6. If your opponent dives on you, do not try to get around the attack but turn to meet it. (this is referred to as "turning the circle" and the pilot whose aircraft is more maneuverable will have the advantage in this).

7. When over enemy lines, always remember your own line of retreat (the Red

Baron was shot down by ground fire while over enemy lines).

8. It is better to attack in groups of four to six. Avoid two aircraft attacking the same opponent (this rule no longer applies because in World War II an American pilot named Thatch developed the "Thatch Weave," a maneuver where two friendly planes crisscross each other's path to snare an enemy in between—Sorry Mr. Boelcke).

Dogfights are called dogfights because of their chaotic nature. Thus, they can be hard to write as any character in the heat of a dogfight will not know entirely what happened on until he gets back to base and can chat it over with his fellow fliers.

A dogfight is a gut-churning, adrenalin-filled battle that is often over in seconds. For this reason, pilots are trained to fall back on rote lessons drilled into them in flight school. There is simply no time to think in complex ways—as the saying goes; "if you think…you're dead."

THE "OODA" LOOP

This funny sounding term applies to any and all combat situations; past, present, and future. US Air Force Colonel Boyd came up with this concept to describe the mental processes of pilots in dogfights. It has since been applied to all military and para-military combat (I first learned it from a police SWAT Team instructor at the Oregon Police Academy).

The loop is composed of four elements:

O—*Observe*
O—*Orient*
D—*Decide*
A—*Act*

In a fight, a warrior must first observe the situation they find themselves in. They must then orient to face their opponent. Next, they must decide how they will handle the situation. Finally, the warrior must act. The warrior will repeat the steps of this loop over and over again as the fight develops. According to Boyd, it is the warrior who can work through these mental steps the fastest who is most likely to win.

These steps must be done in order, simply because that is how the human mind works. Any interruption in the process forces the mind to start all over with "observe." Therefore, anything a warrior can do to distract an opponent is of great tactical value.

As a writer, you can imagine your character going through these steps in combat, whether he is conscious of it or not. Once the first shots are fired, any fight soon becomes a blur of snap judgments and quick reactions. It's usually only after the battles that people are able to piece together what happened in its entirety.

CAVE-MAN STUPID

An old soldier once used this term to describe an aspect of combat to me. The veteran explained that the longer a fight goes on the "stupider" you become because adrenalin soon overwhelms the thought processes.

Moderately complex tasks such as programming a radio or reading a map become extremely difficult and soldiers become "cave-man stupid." The way to counteract this is to make everything as simple as possible before the fight begins.

Each soldier makes sure his extra ammo is kept in the same place on his belt, every time. Weapons are cleaned and maintained after every firefight to be ready the moment the next fight kicks off. Short commands and phrases are used over and over again to be drilled into memory. The more prepared a warrior is, the less he will have to concentrate when he's cave-man stupid.

In this situation, complicated plans are a recipe for disaster. However, even with simple plans, leaders need to make sure every soldier knows their part, inside and out, before the mission begins. In the film, *The Dirty Dozen* the characters learned their attack plan by reciting it in rhyme while their leader pointed to features on a scale model of the building they were to attack. In real life, the soldiers and sailors who participated in the Bin Laden raid practiced on a life-sized mockup of the terrorist's compound so that each man would remember his part under stress.

CONCLUSIONS

Obviously, knowing some tactics will add realism to your military story. Successful soldiers don't just run at the enemy and win by sheer bravado. True, your characters may be brave, but their enemy is sure to be as well. How well your characters can think tactically in battle will go a long way in determining the outcome.

True, often victory goes to the side that simply has the best weapons and the most troops. Dumb luck also plays a part in every military operation. However, a poorly armed small force can defeat a well-armed larger force simply by being more skilled in tactics than their adversary. This is why veteran troops are called "battle-tested," and can be expected to know how to perform under stress much better than any green recruits.

The recruit may think winning involves bravery and nothing more. Dumb luck may even play a part and save the greenhorn in his first fight. But the veteran knows not to count on luck as it favors the enemy as often as not. The veteran understands that bravery is secondary to sound tactics and that tactics involve giving yourself an unfair advantage over your enemy whenever possible.

CHAPTER VII: MILITARY CULTURE

"...We few, we happy few, we band of brothers."

- Shakespeare's Henry V

Every group has a culture; a set of shared values and norms that help its members fit in and work together. The stereotype is that military culture is oppressive, that all soldiers surrender their individuality or have it beaten out of them. And I have read a lot of fiction where soldiers are simply stooges to be outwitted by some smart-ass protagonist. However, as usual, the truth is more nuanced than fiction.

Remember, the US military is made up of hundreds of thousands of people. In any unit, you will meet folks from vastly different parts of the country, different ethnic groups, and vastly different social strata. A variety of personalities that wide is sure to exceed any stereotype. Such an eclectic mix of folks must none the less work together so a new culture is created that everyone can be a part of.

There are common traits to all of the services; such as loyalty and honor. Like the ancient Roman legionnaire, a soldier/sailor/airman/marine must be able to trust that his or her comrade will protect them in battle and know they are on the same side.

Someone who violates that trust through cowardice, incompetence, or treason is sure to be despised by all, especially if a service member dies as a result. As you can well imagine, this kind of tension can help you develop very interesting characters: such as the young marine who is trying to redeem a mistake or the old sergeant who is trying to forgive one. This was the entire theme of a rather famous book titled, *The Four Feathers* by AEW Mason. It's the tale of a man who resigns his army commission to avoid a war. The young man's army buddies subsequently disown him, and he spends the rest of the book trying to reclaim his lost honor—it's worth a read.

Military training is stressful and meant to simulate war. War is extremely stressful, and enough said about that. Strong friendships develop in such circumstances, and many feel they never have, and will never, be as close to any other person as they were to their old military buddies. Of course, this tight-knit community does have its fractures. Military people tend to be highly competitive, playing out in intense rivalries.

In war, we fight the enemy. In peace, we fight each other. The air force pilot who stumbles into a marine bar better be polite and the soldier who makes a navy joke to a SEAL is about to learn a new definition of pain. Every service thinks it's better than the others, and its troops will try to prove that on any and all occasions.

This competitive spirit extends to rivalries between units in the same service. Put a bunch of US Army paratroopers in the same bar with a bunch of US Army Rangers, and you're going to fight. Commanders encourage these rivalries as a way to build their own unit's esprit-de-corps but try to stop short of bar fights and other things likely to get troops in trouble with the military police.

Each service also has its own distinct military culture. The marines are known for iron-hard discipline and strict enforcement of military protocol: you must address sergeants by their exact rank, and always stand at "parade rest" when addressing NCOs (unless you are in the field). The air force can be seen as the opposite end of the spectrum, with a more relaxed climate and an informal attention to military bearing; where any airman can stand comfortably, or even sit when an NCO speaks to him. The army and the navy share places in the middle of that spectrum respectively, with the army being stricter than the navy but often not as strict as the marines.

MILITARY DEATH

Soldiers do not take death lightly. Military funerals are a big deal, and all the services have elaborate rituals to honor the fallen. Such traditions include the slow salute, the riderless horse, the missing man formation, and three rifle casings within a folded American flag. In short, there is no individual whose death means nothing to the rest of his unit. The world of fiction, however, is full of writers that neglect this.

For example, in the classic TV show, *Star Trek*, anonymous crewmen would die left and right while Kirk and company carried on unfazed. This is actually quite offensive, considering the captain would be the one writing the crewman's family a letter of condolence. True, in the middle of a fire-fight you don't have time to mourn the dead, but when the shooting stops, that changes. If a soldier is wounded, extraordinary measures will be put forth to save him. If he dies, his body will be returned to his family if at all possible, even if another soldier has to risk her own life to get it back from the enemy. The movie *Black Hawk Down* directed by Ridley Scott does a good job of portraying this sentiment, and I do recommend it.

POST TRAUMATIC STRESS

As of this writing, the US military has lost more service persons to suicide than combat in Iraq and Afghanistan combined. Now called PTSD, for post-traumatic stress disorder, psychiatric casualties are not new to war. In times past PTSD was called “shell shock” or “battle fatigue.” The stress of battle has always created scars. However, our military culture has always struggled to deal with it appropriately.

Strangely, it’s often the troops who are coolest under fire who are most prone to this condition. In the heat of battle, one must suppress emotions to get the job done. After a soldier leaves the fight, feelings of guilt, remorse, anger, and fear can come bubbling up to the surface. No two people are affected by war the same way, and the symptoms of depression and anxiety may not be immediately recognizable.

In bad writing, soldiers often come home and just “freak out,” exhibiting violent behavior and lashing out at random people (*Rambo: First Blood* by David Morrell). This is not realistic, and I personally find such portrayals offensive. What really happens instead is quite simple. The veteran faces a discord between behaviors that were essential in war but are not relevant in peace. In war, one must be hyper-vigilant and always on the lookout for the smallest sign of danger. But at home, when there is no real danger, habits of war can be hard to unlearn.

For this reason, soldiers coming home often have negative reactions to things once considered normal. For instance, imagine a father driving on the highway. His wife is sitting beside him, and he has an infant son in a baby seat behind him. He passes a wrecked car and is psychologically triggered by memories of a roadside bomb exploding in Iraq. Although he may show no outward sign initially, adrenalin spikes as his body prepares for flight or fight.

The vet is now keenly alert to the slightest sign of danger while his wife continues to enjoy the scenery out the passenger window. Suddenly, the baby in the back seat cries out because he dropped a toy. Dad screams at the kid to shut up. He's looking for the enemy for god's sake, why would anybody cry out at a time like this?

His wife comes to her child's defense; after all, he's just a baby who dropped a toy. This, in turn, sets off one hell of an argument. By the time all the shouting is done, the veteran doesn't remember what triggered him in the first place—he just feels terrible that he yelled at his wife and child. That is what a typical PTSD event looks like, and soldiers have dealt with it throughout history.

Sadly, today, those who know psychiatric help is available often don't try to get it for fear of being considered "weak." The military has a rather machismo mindset, and that is simply not the best approach to these problems. Veterans suffering from PTSD who don't get help often turn to alcohol (which is acceptable in military culture) or street drugs (which aren't). As of right now, the military is trying to change its ways so that seeking proper treatment for PTSD is more acceptable.

Unfortunately, sometimes the hardest things to change are people's minds.

MILITARY JARGON

You can add realism to your writing by throwing in some military phraseology. Today, it mostly consists of a long list of three-letter acronyms. Al Qaeda in Iraq was AQI; sergeants are NCOs, your dinner is an

MRE (***M***eal ***R***eady to ***E***at), and so on. These acronyms are always changing and are beyond the scope of this, or any other, book.

The navy and marines take it one step further by attempting to re-write the entire English language; stairways are always called ladders, floors are decks, walls are bulkheads. Hell, sailors can't even say "yes" to an officer. They have to say "aye," and they have to say it twice to indicate they both heard and will comply with an order.

"Aye-aye, Sir, I will swab the deck and clean the bulkheads."

Much of contemporary military language evolved from the need to be understood over crackling radios.

Here are some radio terms that are often used out of habit, even when troops are not talking on a radio.

Roger—*"I heard and understood you."*

Over—*"I am done talking and ready to listen."*

Out—*"Our conversation is done."*

Say again—*"I want you to repeat what you just said."*

Repeat—*Only used when talking to artillery troops, and means you want them to blast the same location again.*

Copy that—*I understood you and/or agree with you.*

Due to this need for clarity letters and numbers are pronounced in a specific way.

1—One *6—Six*

2—Two *7—Seven*
3—Tree (not a typo) *8—Eight*
4—Four *9—Niner*
5—Fife (not a typo) *10—One-Zero*

When saying numbers above nine, each digit is stated separately. For instance: the number thirty is pronounced tree-zero, forty-five is four-fife, and so on.

Please note the usage of "over and out" is improper radio protocol. When a character says "over" they're telling the other person, they are done talking and are ready to listen, but when they say "out" that means the conversation is done, and they wouldn't necessarily hear a reply anyway.

Letters are spoken as follows.

A—Alpha	*N—November*
B—Bravo	*O—Oscar*
C—Charlie	*P—Papa*
D—Delta	*Q—Quebec*
E—Echo	*R—Romeo*
F—Foxtrot	*S—Sierra*
G—Gulf	*T—Tango*
H—Hotel	*U—Uniform*
I—India	*V—Victor*
J—Juliet	*W—Whiskey*
K—Kilo	*X—X-ray*
L—Lima	*Y—Yankee*
M—Mike	*Z—Zulu*

Thus, a soldier in "C company" will refer to his unit as "Charlie Company."

Military time is always referred to using the twenty-four-hour clock. This means that 1:00pm in the civilian's world is referred to as 1300 hours by the soldier. This can prevent a lot of problems in battle. If a general told his troops to attack at 4:30, he may get half his troops attacking in the early morning hour of 0430, and the other half joining the fight at 1630 hours, so he is sure to be more specific.

There are two words of modern military jargon every writer should include. They are derived from the ancient British cheer "huzzah." These uniquely American words are used to signify everything but "no." As such, they are the most useful words in the entire English language…and they sound like cavemen grunting.

HOOAH! - The Army word for everything but no.

OOHRAH! - The Marine Corps word for everything but no.

Soldiers and marines will shout these words whenever the situation calls for a cheer or word of strong affirmation.

Profanity is also common in the military, and it is the unusual service member who doesn't cuss. Even in days gone by, American Civil War soldiers were observed to be more profane than the rules of polite society allowed. It is also not uncommon in the military for a superior to cuss out a subordinate, and any complaint is likely to fall on deaf ears unless racial or gender discriminatory terms are involved.

Of final note, the word "gun" is used differently in the military than in the civilian world. A gun refers to a cannon specifically, and no weapon of smaller size can be called by that term. Thus, no soldier carries a gun into battle (unless the man's first name is King and his last name is Kong). Instead, soldiers carry "weapons." Sometimes these weapons are referred to using their proper names such as rifles, machine guns, or pistols, but they are never called guns.

THE SCROUNGER

There is one type of character no military unit should be without. It is not an official job, however, and never will be. Still, I'm sure every unit has had one since Caesar crossed the Rubicon—it's the scrounger. They may not be the best soldiers in the unit, but nobody minds because they can get anything needed whether the unit is supposed to have it or not.

True, troops are supplied through the regular military logistical system. However, that system can be inflexible and cannot provide everything needed in time. Low on bullets or fuel and don't have time to screw around? Go get the scrounger!

Scroungers live by a simple code: if their unit needs it, they will get it—legally or not. Scroungers can be seen making deals to trade items between units, or they might be spotted looting burned out vehicles for spare parts. Occasionally, a scrounger may acquire some other unit's property that has been left, shall we say, unguarded. Such a character is likely to think of himself more as a "wheeler-dealer" than a thief…but sometimes a thief.

PATRIOTISM

Although touched on before, this point bears repeating. Military people are very patriotic. When the day ends, bugle calls are broadcast on speakers throughout most every base. Soldiers and sailors will turn to the sound of the music and salute the flag, even when no one is watching. When a movie is played in a military theater, the national anthem precedes it, and the audience will all rise. True military people are paid to serve. But no one is willing to die for a dollar. But they will die, if necessary, for a cause. In the case of the US military, that cause is patriotism.

That being said, soldiers who spend little time among civilians often experience a kind of culture clash when home on leave.

Soldiers often feel a discord between themselves and their less patriotic fellow citizens who have not sworn their life to the nation's defense. Depending on the personalities involved, this can lend drama, tragedy or comedy to your story. Civilians may idolize the military or disparage it, but seldom do they truly understand it.

STOLEN VALOR

This is a huge problem in America today—the false claim of military service. Perhaps it's due to all the attention veterans coming home from Iraq and Afghanistan are getting today that some folks just feel inadequate and start telling lies to make themselves sound heroic. Recently, it has even been made a federal crime to falsely claim military service if you benefit financially from it. That being said, lying to impress a girl is still completely legal.

I consider there to be two types of valor thieves. They are the outright lair and the embellisher.

The first one is easier to spot. The outright liar never actually served in the military at all. Everything he knows, he learned from movies, books, and the internet. He is want to make outlandish claims about the medals he supposedly earned, the missions that he professes to have been on and the fighting he was never in. Some even go so far as to but medals at a surplus store and wear them incorrectly on uniforms procured at the same place. When confronted with the inconsistencies of their tales, they often double down on their lie. They do this by claiming they were on "secret missions" and can't produce the proof because it's "classified."

The embellisher is a guy who actually served in the military but never did the things he claims. Such a person may have been dishonorably discharged or simply feels inadequate for some other reason. I was once taken in by a guy who claimed to have been a jet fighter pilot in Vietnam. When I asked him for details about his service, he became increasingly vague. So I looked up his record and found he'd been an electrician on an aircraft carrier during the Vietnam War, but never flew a plane.

CHAPTER VIII: OUR FRIENDS AND FRENEMIES

Naturally, the US military isn't alone in the world. We have our friends, our enemies and, well, our frenemies. Our most reliable friends are the NATO allies (the North Atlantic Treaty Organization). As to enemies, of late we've been at war with terrorist groups and other kinds of irregular fighters that are covered in a later chapter. However, our frenemies are a bit harder to nail down. These are countries that we rival but have no current hostilities with such as China.

Fair to say, each nation has its own peculiar military customs and structures, and it is well beyond the scope of this book to cover them all. However, it can be helpful to get a feel for some of the differences and similarities if your story involves troops of more than one nation, so here goes.

GREAT BRITAIN

The United Kingdom is, without a doubt, America's most supportive military friend. Since World War II, we regularly conduct joint training with the Brits, and they have fought alongside us in Iraq and Afghanistan. I once got to know a British Army warrant officer while serving in Iraq, and I learned some interesting things.

First off, this royal warrant officer wore a US sergeant major's emblem on his shirt so all the bloody Americans could figure out where he stood on the totem pole. It seems the Brits have only four kinds of sergeant (as opposed to our five), and thus our sergeant majors are roughly equivalent to their warrant officers.

Another oddity of the land of tea and crumpets is that British Army units all recruit from assigned geographical areas. Thus, every member of a regiment will be from roughly the same hometown. Such a regiment is comprised of two parts, the active duty half, and the territorial half. The active-duty troops can be anywhere in the world, but the territorial soldiers stay in the regiment's hometown and function a lot like the American army reserves or national guard.

Keep in mind that in the age of Queen Victoria—one-third of the nations of the world were under the rule of the British Empire. Thus, many a nation's militaries are based on the British model in terms of rank and structure.

You can also expect soldiers from Australia, Canada, and New Zealand to stand up straight when the band plays *"God Save The Queen.* Soldiers from India and South Africa, however, might give a polite nod.

FRANCE

Interestingly, at the time Great Britain was our greatest enemy, France was our greatest friend. It was French support for the American Revolution that gave us a fighting chance at independence. When the French Navy successfully blockaded Yorktown in 1781, the Brits were forced to surrender to Washington. However, that was a long time ago.

Sadly, many American soldiers today view the French as weak and unstable allies. The reason dates back to World War II when France was completely overrun by the Germans in a matter of weeks. Subsequently, during the Nazi occupation, many French people collaborated with the Germans, which also affected American opinions. To be fair, many French fought heroically in the French resistance, or as part of the Free French Forces which took part in the battle of D-Day.

After World War II, things got bad for the French Empire and their military star continued to plummet. Famously, they were driven out of Vietnam by the communists, which led to the eventual US involvement in that war.

The icing on the cake for the current generation of American soldiers was the French refusal to participate in the Iraq War. This prompted much anti-French sentiment in the early 2000’s despite the fact the French were fighting alongside US forces in Afghanistan at the time.

To be clear, the French are not weak.

Today, they are often found fighting in Africa against Jihadist militias or serving as part of UN peacekeeping efforts. For these missions, the French often deploy one of the oldest and most respected units in the world, the French Foreign Legion. With a very colorful history, this unique organization is great fodder for any writer.

Founded in 1831, the Legion is made up of foreigners from every part of the globe, such as: Germans, Irishmen, Americans, and others. Therefore, they are not French soldiers at all but rather mercenaries in French employ. In the 1800s, the Foreign Legion was the hammer of French imperialism. The French Empire was a big place and in those days, and the Legion was often sent to lonely outposts in the deserts of North Africa.

Today, the Foreign Legion is France's rapid-response troops. They are sent to world trouble spots on a moment's notice to secure French interests, and they are damn good at the job. Men who join the Legion (and it is an all-male force) do so for a five-year tour. During that time, they assume false names, and it is considered the height of rudeness to ask a legionnaire about his past.

After their five-year tour is up, the veteran legionnaires become French citizens under their new name and identity. Naturally, this has a great appeal for a man on the run who needs a place to hide. In times past, it was not uncommon for the scum of Europe to run to the Legion's door, seeking sanctuary. Along with criminals, the Legion's ranks contained failed revolutionaries, poets, and the semi-suicidal. Today, the Legion claims it no longer accepts wanted criminals but is willing to overlook "something that proves you're a man"–whatever that means.

THE RUSSIANS

Once our greatest rival, the Russian military has an old and storied history. It was the Russians defeat of Napoleon's army in 1812 that inspired the great overture of that name (not the American War of 1812, sorry). The Russians fought in both world wars against Germany, and in each one, they suffered incredible hardships.

The brutal conditions Russian soldiers faced in those wars shaped much of their military culture today. For a movie that shows the Eastern Front of World War II, I recommend *Enemy at the Gates,* starring Jude Law, and *Defiance,* starring Daniel Craig. But a warning, both of these movies can be hard to watch.

In Iraq, I once met an Estonian soldier (now part of NATO). This guy had served his country for a long time and was a young soldier back when there was an "Iron Curtain." I noticed he wore the blue and white striped undershirt of Russia's elite soldiers, the Spetsnaz. I asked him about it, and the Estonian admitted with pride he had attended Soviet Spetsnaz training in the late 1980s.

I asked what the training was like. He answered, "It was okay, but I did not like running in the fear." When asked what "running in the fear" meant. The Estonian told me that Spetsnaz candidates would run several kilometers a day, and in the back of the formation was a Russian sergeant with a rifle. If a soldier failed to keep up with the running formation, the sergeant would beat them with the butt of the rifle. Thus, the soldiers "ran in fear" because a man with a gun was literally chasing them.

Brutality like that is not accepted in the US military, but it's just another day at the office for the Spetsnaz. Their reputation for brutality to others is also legendary. In actions as recent as the Chechen War of 1999 to 2000, Spetsnaz instilled terror in their enemies without apparent remorse: 25,000 people killed and 5,000 people "disappeared."

Generally speaking, Russian technology is behind ours, but with a well-funded and well-disciplined military, they could still pose a threat to American interests in the future. Thus, despite the collapse of the Soviet Union, the Russians are still considered a formidable rival to US military power...a frenemy.

IRAQ

Oh boy, friend or frenemy…where do I begin? The Iraqi Army has historically been the glue that held Iraqi society together, which means it also, has been the club that beat that society into line. In fact, "Army Day" (January six) is as great an Iraqi national holiday as the American's Independence Day (July four). Formed during the British occupation of the 1920s, the Iraqi Army models itself along British organizational lines in terms of rank and structure. After that, well, it's interesting.

During the regime of Saddam Hussein, the Iraqi Army included an organization known as the Republican Guard. Ostensibly an elite unit for national defense, its true purpose was to protect the regime against coup attempts. The Republican Guard was better paid, better trained, and better equipped than the rest of the army, and to get into it a soldier had to prove he was totally loyal to the regime.

Rumor has it, one such loyalty test involved masked men bursting into a soldier's room at night. The masked men told the soldier this was a coup, and they were overthrowing Saddam Husain. The men then told the soldier if he wished to live he must join the coup. If the soldier said he was loyal to Saddam he passed the test—if the soldier said he was willing to join the coup to save his life, he was shot dead on the spot.

After the US invasion, the Iraqi Army was disbanded by American appointee Paul Bremer. Much has been said about how stupid it was to render thousands of armed and trained men unemployed all at once, and I need not elaborate here. A new Iraqi Army was trained and equipped by the US to be our ally in the region, but with friends like this…

As of my last overseas tour in 2011, the Iraqi Army wasn't very impressive. The Shia (a sect of Islam) majority was in charge of the newly elected government, and by "coincidence" only Shia officers seemed to be running things. The Iraqi Sunnis (another sect of Islam) were pushed onto the sidelines and treated with suspicion at best. Nepotism ran rampant in the Iraqi army, and a soldier's family/tribal connections were a much surer path to promotion than competence. For example, Iraqi's elite mechanized division was commanded by the president's cousin. Coincidence? I think not.

Iraqi sergeants were given little or no

responsibility, and the officers were tied up with even the most trivial details. In fact, my interpreter often let Iraqis assume I was an American captain (I wore civilian clothes) because if the Iraqis knew they were dealing with a sergeant, they'd give me no respect. Naturally, impersonating an officer is an offense that could have gotten me in big trouble, so I'm glad my interpreter told me about it after the fact.

Iraqi army officers were poorly paid but nonetheless found creative ways to increase their income. An Iraqi enlisted man who wished to stay home could pay his captain half of his enlisted salary, and in return, the captain would keep the soldier on the books in good standing. Later, after I returned home, I heard how the Iraqi soldiers ran from the Islamic militants who call themselves the "Islamic State." I wasn't surprised in the least. Would you follow a captain into battle that you'd been paying off for the past few years?

It is unfair to say all developing nations have such a low level of military professionalism, and it is possible the Iraqi Army will temper in the fire of its battle with radical jihadists. However, writers who wish to set their story in such places would be mistaken to assume American military competency is common throughout the world.

CHAPTER IX: NON-TRADITIONAL SOLDIERS

MILITIA GROUPS

Militias are to the military what posses are to law enforcement. They are small groups of a couple of hundred people or less, who carry guns and believe in some common cause. After that, they can be quite a motley crew.

Once part of American life from the time of the first colonies, militias used to be made up of every fighting-aged, free white male in a country, and would report to the county's courthouse one day every month to practice marching and shooting. These folks became politically active in the late 1700s and formed the basis of George Washington's Continental Army. However, they were still a motley crew and had some rather bad habits (like running away from the enemy). Only later in our revolution did the militiamen become soldiers, and more on that later.

Keep in mind the US lost most of the battles in our revolution!

Militias still exist today, and they are still motley crews. They are found in Afghanistan, Somalia, and other hot-spots around the world. In Iraq, our main threat came from such groups with names such as Asa'ib Ahl al-Haq (The League of the Righteous), or Jaish al-Mahdi (The Army of the Messiah). However, we also had success with our own militias during a period known as the Anbar Awakening. Apparently, Iraqis were fed up with Al Qaeda and asked for US help to drive them out of Anbar province. The US Army gave the Iraqis some money and yellow reflective belts (no kidding), so we would know who the good guys were. The Anbar militias did the rest.

There are also modern militias in America; the Second Amendment mentions "a well-ordered militia being necessary…". And some folks actually go out and form one. In my home state of Oregon, we recently had a militia group occupy the Malheur National Wildlife Refuge. It caused quite a stir, and as of this writing, the participants are awaiting trial.

Most militias can be described as improvised bands of true believers, who have little training and often-questionable leadership. Weapons are of a mixed type and often use different kinds of ammunition so troops can't help each other when one guy runs out of bullets. Uniforms in militias usually don't exist (unless somebody gives them reflective belts), and they are often paid exactly like a Roman Legionnaire.

Famously undisciplined, militiamen are often found sleeping on guard duty, and when awake they are easily bribed anyway. With all this said about how bad militias are, a soldier must always keep in mind they can kill. Underestimating a large group of armed folks is never a good idea, and occasionally, they win.

A fact Great Britain still remembers.

MERCENARIES

A mercenary, or soldier of fortune if you prefer, is a soldier for hire and they have existed for a very long time. The Romans hired foreign tribes to act as scouts and auxiliary troops, and it was good business for the times.

The US's most famous foreign hire was, without a doubt a mercenary named Barron Von Steuben. When General Washington got tired of losing battles, he hired a German officer to train and organize the American militia into the Continental Army. Von Steuben formed our troops into regular units with regular tactics, military discipline, and a formal rank structure. Being from Germany, Von Steuben spoke no English and did all his work through a translator, including his textured and rich use of profanity.

Naturally, mercenaries still exist and probably will into the distant future. America's use of private security companies, such as Blackwater in Iraq, is a clear example or our use of 'mercs in modern times. In 2011, I worked in Iraq with mercenary companies like The Olive Group and Tiger Swan who provided security as the US drew down its regular forces.

Such modern mercenaries are mostly ex-soldiers from somebody's army (sometimes even ours). They take jobs as they come; from bodyguard work to convoy escorts, to the rescue of kidnap victims. Their outlook on life is military, and they form companies that are structured with military rank and discipline in mind. But, keep in mind this is just a job to a mercenary. He does not always care about the cause he is fighting for, so long as he gets paid and maintains a professional reputation. He is often willing to kill for an employer but is seldom willing to die for one.

POLITICAL SOLDIERS

Except for a debacle involving a Civil War general named Freemont, the US has never had political soldiers (by the way, the "Freemont Bodyguard" didn't last long). Despite this one historical exception, American soldiers do not take an oath to any specific person, political party or faction of the government. American servicemen and women swear an oath to the constitution and the leaders that are appointed over them by law.

Political soldiers are quite a different animal.

From the Roman Emperor's Praetorians to Saddam Hussein's Republican Guard, troops of this kind have existed chiefly to prop up dictators and oppress their own people. The two most well-known examples of modern times are the Nazi SS and Soviet Commissars.

The Nazi SS was the evilest bunch of sons of bitches the world has ever seen. These were the goons that ran Hitler's concentration camps and murdered civilians by the millions. They were an elite unit of soldiers who were given the best training, equipment, food, and pay Nazi Germany could provide. They were chosen for "racial purity" and wore special black uniforms that distinguished them from the rest of the German army.

The Commissars of the Soviet Union operated very differently. During the Russian Civil War, it was often hard to tell which side specific units were on because those units kept changing loyalties. The communist government was weak and unable to manage all the disparate elements of its Red Army and needed a way to exert control.

The solution was to assign special soldiers to each unit whose loyalty to the communist cause was beyond question: the commissars. Commissars taught the troops communist values and encouraged them to obey their commander. If the commander acted in a way that was not good for the communist party, the commissar would shoot that commander dead, and then appoint a new commander.

Commissars often employed spies among the troops who reported on their fellows to prevent mutiny as well as treachery. Those accused went to prison or worse, often without trial. This brutal system worked very well and continued long after the revolution succeeded.

REBELS

Throughout history, there have been rebels fighting against their own government. Most rebellions fail, but hey, some get lucky. Historically, there have been two basic structures of rebel armies, and they are determined by the force's origin. So ask yourself, writer, is your rebel force top-down or bottom-up?

A top-down rebellion is lead by the people who are near the highest pinnacles of society. Both the American Revolution and the Confederate rebellion of southern states followed this model. The leaders of local communities decided that the people running things in the faraway capital had to go. So, they organized every asset the community possessed to that cause and went to war. Top-down rebellions fight with fairly regular armies that often wear uniforms and are issued weapons by the rebel government.

Bottom-up rebellions are usually started when a small bunch of people decides things have gone far enough, and take it unto themselves to do something about it. These are idealists with a passion for a cause but no real resources. These groups often steal what they need (as in the bank robberies of the SLA in the 1970s), and hope not to be discovered by police until "the time is right." The communist revolutions of the 20th century were such "bottom-up" enterprises.

A classic example of a successful bottom-up rebellion is Castro. He and a small band of followers snuck into Cuba in an old yacht and trekked to the mountains. They organized the mountain peasants into an army and fought from there.

Bottom-up rebellions don't have the resources to organize regular armies and instead fight with crude militias. Often the intellectuals have no real military experience, which leads to some quality "out of the box thinking" on some days, and some real disasters on others. Such a group will be happy for the help of a professional soldier, but will also be wary of him. After all, he might be a police spy!

TERRORISTS

The saying goes, "one man's terrorist is another man's freedom fighter"—horse crap. Terrorists are defined by their tactics not who's side they are on.

As the title implies, the goal of a terrorist is to spread terror among the people he's decided are his enemies. Once his victims are afraid, the terrorist can use that fear to break down their faith in the legitimate government until it no longer protects them—because they believe it can't!

Terrorists seldom strike at military targets, and to them, a shopping mall is often a better place to attack than an army base. Firstly, the mall is bound to be less guarded than a base, so the chances of getting away with it are much better. Secondly, a mall has more people in a smaller area, and the bomb will, therefore, cause more human suffering. This will surely get the terrorist's attack on the news and send fear rippling throughout the nation.

Unfortunately, these tactics often work. By committing a large number of very violent attacks in a short space and time, citizens begin to believe their government cannot protect them. They may call 911 and get yet another busy signal. When that happens, people often start to take matters into their own hands. This leads to riots and civil disorder that breaks the already strained civil services and security system.

With police overwhelmed, the military is often called in to "do something." The problem is, most military units are not trained for this situation and don't know what to do.

In the chaos, the terrorists attempt to replace the legitimate government. They rarely can do this, however, since leading people is always a lot harder than killing people. A good movie on this subject is *Michel Collins* starring Liam Neeson. The film portrays the Irish Revolution of the early 20th century and the invention of such tactics by the Irish Republican Army.

A terrorist group's worst enemy is a civilian population unwilling to provide support or, even worse, willing to expose them. To counter this inclination, terrorists often provide services to the people to gain popular support. Many Middle Eastern groups offer charitable services to poor neighborhoods or operate schools in remote areas that are otherwise unserved.

Terrorists are usually best confronted by spies, who discover their hiding places and weapons' caches. Elite squads of commandos can then take them out. Unfortunately, such spies need time to work, and the commandos may be off fighting a war overseas. In short, terrorists can be a real pain in the butt.

PART B: LAW ENFORCEMENT

CHAPTER X: POLICE HISTORY

"Each man's business is the Kings. But each man's soul is his own."
-William Shakespeare, Henry the V

Enforcing the law in the days of sword and spear was done by order of the king as carried out by his loyal officers and subjects. In the British Norman tradition, the king appointed a "constable" to manage each castle or similarly walled town, and a "reeve" to collect taxes in every shire.

The constables chiefly concerned themselves with defending the king's fortresses and were given charge of men-at-arms to that purpose. But of course, the enemy was not always at the gates and crime within the walls of a city could be quite a threat by itself. So, townspeople would often come to the constable and ask him to arrest some miscreant who caused trouble since he had the troops to do it and the duty to maintain order within the walls.

A shire is a loosely defined farming community that is typically larger than a village but smaller than a county. The shire's reeve, or sheriff for short, collected taxes, and when people couldn't pay, he placed them in "debtor's prisons" until some friend or relation coughed up the cash. As the sheriff also had an armed group of bodyguards (tax collectors are seldom popular fellows), he too would be called upon to arrest troublemakers. Or in the case of one Robin of Loxley, he at least tried to.

And yes, I know the jury is still out regarding the historical Robin Hood.

Either constable's guard or sheriff's soldier would be armed as any man-at-arms of the day, but they weren't the only "cops" on the beat. Any subject of the king, from yeoman farmer to blacksmith, also had the right and duty to make an arrest. In towns, homeowners were often made to walk around the village at night to watch out for trouble. These "town watchmen" had absolutely no training of any kind but, nevertheless, were charged to do this as a civic duty. If a night watchman carried any weapon at all, it would be his own club or dagger, and he probably couldn't afford armor.

A comic example of the town's night watch is found in Shakespeare's comedy *Much Ado About Nothing*, a movie version was made in 1993 featuring Michael Keeton as Dogberry, the incompetent town constable, and I highly recommend it.

As amateurish as the town watchman sounds, things often became less formal than even that. All too commonly, a mob of common people would decide a certain person's behavior had finally caused enough trouble, and they would hunt the fellow down and drag him to court.

By "court" it was typically meant the nearest representative of the king such as a local knight or baron. Without lawyers or formal proceedings, the noble would hear the case and decide the fate of the accused. Of course, justice then, as now, isn't exactly blind. If the mob was strong and the nobleman weak the sentence could be a foregone conclusion.

"Trial by combat" was also an option,

but only for an accused nobleman. In such a "trial," the accused would fight against a knightly opponent, and it would be assumed that God himself would ensure the right prevailed. A similar notion was "trial by ordeal," which involved such novel ideas as placing a hot coal in the accused's palm. If he were innocent, God would not let his flesh burn—right?

Punishment for lesser crimes usually involved a few days locked in the stocks. This was meant to deter further crime by public example and to shame the offender. More serious crimes led to fines or periods of incarceration in whatever lock-up was available. Seldom were people given long prison sentences in the Middle Ages, as there simply wasn't a long-term prison system in place. Perhaps for this reason, death was a common punishment for crimes such as robbery, treason, rape, or murder.

The problems with this system should be obvious. The law enforcers had no special training in the law, and the accused could easily be put to death on trumped up charges like witchcraft. Also, it would be a poor decision for a lower class watchman to accuse a noble lord of any crime whatsoever unless compelled by absolute necessity—these were not egalitarian times.

Often, the law served the king's interest first and the people, who were victims of crime, hardly at all. And speaking of the king, he was likely miles away, having no idea how often his officials took bribes or if they actually enforced his laws in the first place.

Of course, this is all meat food for a writer to chew on. For a good murder mystery set in the historical Middle Ages, I recommend the *Brother Cadfael* books by Ellis Peters. They give a real insight into the problems of properly enforcing the law, without the aid of any modern notions of evidence or due process. For a good laugh, I can also recommend *Guards! Guards!* by Terry Pratchett. This book and others by Mr. Prachett, depict law enforcement in a fantasy world rife with good jokes and stinging social commentary.

VICTORIAN AGE COPPERS

"Brass buttons, blue coat, couldn't catch a nanny goat!"

- Children's taunt from Boston's south side, circa 1840

Now, I'll jump ahead in time a few hundred years to the Industrial Revolution. As common people began gaining more and more political power, the profession of law enforcement became more and more professional.

But not all at once.

The first major change was the creation of actual police departments. An English statesman named Robert Peel can be rightly said to be the pioneer in this field. While serving as Britain's Home Secretary, he established London's Metropolitan Police Force in 1829. His three "Peelian Principals" would guide law enforcement to this day, and it is sad to report when they are not adhered to.

The principals of Mr. Peel were as follows:

1. Every police officer should be issued a badge number, to assure accountability for his actions.

2. Whether the police are effective is measured not by the number of arrests, but on the lack of crime.

3. Above all else, an effective authority figure is known and trusted. His accountability is paramount.

Incidentally, it is for Mr. *Robert* Peel that British policemen are called "bobbies" to this day. In America, they were called "coppers," and the origin of that slang is a bit less clear. Some suggest it is for the cheap copper badges they once wore or the term may be a corruption of the phrase "to cop," meaning "to take," as in to "take a criminal into custody."

Nicknames aside, professional policemen were something new in the world—uniformed men, without military duties, who existed solely to enforce the law.

The uniform was important because it was generally the only thing issued besides billy-clubs. Guns were seldom issued to early officers, and it was not uncommon for a constable to buy his own pistol for protection. And that early constable might well need protection because he had no way of calling for help except to shout or blow his whistle and hope another copper heard him.

Once the telephone was invented, in 1876, "police call boxes" (that looked exactly like the exterior of Dr. Who's time machine) were placed throughout most major cities. The call box was just a phone booth with a light on top and a locked door. When the light flashed, a cop walking his beat would run to unlock the door and answer the phone. The officer would then find out where the trouble was and run off to meet it. Policemen were also expected to call the station periodically to check in while walking their beats. The 1944 film *Arsenic and Old Lace* has a scene where a policeman asks the homeowner if he can borrow her phone to check in with his sergeant, and it's taken as a common practice by everyone concerned.

The old Victorian cops attended no formal police academy and were not particularly well schooled in the law. Indeed, they were often selected simply because they were tough-looking fellows who could handle themselves in a fight. After the New York draft riots of 1863, pistols were introduced. However, without training that probably didn't work out too well. In fact, by order of Police Commissioner Theodore Roosevelt, the city of New York opened America's first police academy in 1895—for the training of marksmanship, not law.

To compensate for the constable's legal ignorance, special judges called "magistrates," were created. When a crook was dragged, bruised and bleeding, in front of such a magistrate, the tale would be told. Once the magistrate heard both the cop and the crook's story, he would decide if the policeman had acted correctly. If the cop was right, the miscreant went to jail to await trial. If the cop was wrong, the citizen walked free. Charles Dickens gives an example of this kind of justice in *Oliver*

Twist when Oliver is arrested for pick-pocketing, and the magistrate is drunk.

Now for some really bad news, these old time cops were almost always connected to "the machine." In the 1800's most American city governments were run by "machine politicians," corrupt mafia types who often cheated to get elected so they could steal money from the city's coffers. These scheming politicians often had humble beginnings. They came from poor neighborhoods and depended on "friends" to help them gain office. Naturally, after they got elected, they were expected to reward their friends with city employment.

Like police jobs.

It so happens there is a stereotype that all cops are Irish (watch old Bugs Bunny cartoons if you don't believe me). The truth is, for various reasons, Irish immigrant communities were especially skilled at machine politics. With one ethnic group in control of the city and its police, it doesn't take a lot of writer imagination to see how they could lord it over others. Needless to say, an Irish criminal had a better chance of avoiding arrest than an offender of Italian,

Jewish, or African descent.

Here is another bit of bad news: even though the police were patronage jobs, they were poorly paid patronage jobs. The fat cats, like the "Tammany Hall" gang, were at city hall stealing cash right from the treasury, so few scraps fell from that table. What's a poor cop to do? Well, let's just say if a character in your story is arrested for "attempted bribery"—it's likely he didn't offer the copper enough dough.

Still, there are always honest people that just want to support their families while doing some good in the world. Indeed, the one hero cop on a bad force can indeed make for a very interesting character—if he lives long enough.

WILD WEST SHERIFFS

Following the English medieval model, every county in America had a sheriff. This person is elected by the people—the theory being if he turns out to be corrupt, the people will just toss him out in the next election. For this reason, the sheriff is considered the supreme law enforcement official in his county, and in the old days, he was the only one who got paid a salary for his trouble.

Now, a man has got to make a living, and nobody is born a sheriff. This brings up the relevant question of what the person did before they were elected.

In the old west, sheriffs were often prominent citizens, such as mill owners or ranchers. Chances are they didn't sell the mill when they got elected either. This type of sheriff was basically a part-time lawman. He still had his business to run, and his official duties necessarily came in second place to keeping his true livelihood afloat.

There was also the not so prominent citizen who got elected sheriff. Former cattle rustlers and gunfighters often got the job due to their, shall we say, familiarity with crime. How did these men get elected? Prominent citizens helped them of course. Prominent citizens, who did not want to leave their business but simply wanted that business protected by an efficient killer wearing a badge.

One of the greatest western movies ever made is *Silverado,* starring Danny

Glover, and it tells the fictional tale of such a situation. Naturally, in the film, a bunch of brave and honest cowboys rides into town to take out the corrupt lawman and his prominent citizen boss. Personally, I highly recommend this film for those who wish to understand the formula of a traditional American western.

DEPUTIES, POSSIES AND TOWN MARSHALS

Sheriffs would often hire deputies to assist with their duties. A deputy took an oath to the law exactly like the sheriff and had all of the sheriff's legal powers. A deputy received no regular salary or hourly pay. Instead, deputies were paid a certain rate for each warrant served, prisoner escorted or criminal captured. Naturally, there were few lazy deputies.

When an especially heinous crime was committed, a posse would be formed of every armed farmer and ranch hand that wanted to find a specific criminal and bring him to justice. Often, a posse was a hard-to-control mob of rugged, armed, and possibly inebriated, individuals who just wanted a share in the reward or to lynch the wrongdoer outright. In short, this could be one dangerous bunch of yahoos.

Occasionally, you hear of sheriffs forming posses today, usually when there is a search for a missing person or similar effort that needs a lot of manpower to comb through remote areas for evidence (drunken yahoos need not apply).

The town marshals of the old west were policemen employed by the town government. There usually weren't many of them, and they were often as poorly paid as the big city police officer. Hiring criteria could be rather informal, and family relations could help secure such a job. One such group of marshals worked for the town of Tombstone, Arizona. You may have already heard of them, and they were all related—the Earp brothers.

The gunfight at the OK Corral was, of course, their most famous moment. It is worthy to note, that the county sheriff was also in Tombstone at the time of the great shootout. The sheriff, however, was not involved in that gunfight. Because it seems, he and the Earps didn't get along. The Earp's best friend on that day was actually the town dentist who helped out with a shotgun. His name was Holliday, and he had no legal authority whatsoever.

TEXAS RANGERS

Texas began life as a part of Mexico. Immigrants from the United States were allowed in to settle there on three conditions: 1) they promise to be good citizens of Mexico, 2) they could not bring slavery with them, and 3) they had to become members of the Catholic Church. Predictably, the settlers did none of the above and soon revolted. After a disastrous battle at The Alamo followed by a victory by the San Jacinto River, Texas became an independent country in 1836. It later joined the United States 1846, and its president then became its governor.

The new Texas nation had no army or police, so they created a force that would serve as both, the rangers. Rangers were given large tracts of land to patrol and seldom traveled in groups much larger than twenty. They were appointed by the president, and later the governor, of Texas. They provided their own horses, weapons and even had to make their own badges (out of Mexican silver dollars).

The Texas Rangers now exist as a kind of elite police force exclusive to Texas. Acting as special investigators, they assist local police departments and sheriffs' offices upon request. There is also an Arizona Rangers that performs the same role in the next state over. Rangers are still appointed by the state governor, and those appointments are very hard to get.

CHAPTER XI: FEDERAL LAW ENFORCEMENT

THE FEDERAL MARSHALS

Richard Kimble: I didn't kill my wife!
Deputy Marshal Gerard: I don't care.
-The Fugitive (1993)

Before statehood, areas like Kansas, Dakota, Oregon, and Nebraska were governed from Washington DC as US territories. To enforce the law, Federal Courts dispatched Federal Marshals. Back then, citizens often traveled days to the courthouse to complain about some troublemaker. The judge would then write out a warrant for that suspect's arrest and send a marshal out to get him.

The marshal then sought out the outlaw and attempted to bring him back to the courthouse to face trial. This is, of course, not untrodden ground for a writer. The book that became the movie *True Grit*, starring John Wayne, involves the exploits of such a marshal, and I recommend the book, the original movie, and even the remake.

Once the prisoner was sentenced, the marshal would be responsible for taking that inmate to a federal prison—usually in Ft. Leavenworth, Kansas or Detroit, Michigan. The journeys of marshals to take prisoners safely to prison also makes great stuff for old west adventures as the prisoner may attempt to escape, or his old enemies may try to lynch him.

Today, the US Marshals still do that same job. They work out of federal courthouses and are still responsible for federal inmates. Interestingly, a rather bizarre task of today's U.S. Marshals is the supervision of the Witness Protection Program, as a result of the Organized Crime Control Act of 1970.

When someone testifies against organized crime in Federal Court, there is usually a price to pay. The mob will want those "squealers" dead, and this tends to discourage folks from testifying in the first place. The Witness Protection Program gives these people a new identity, right down to a new birth certificate and social security number. This allows the witness to hide from the mob and start a new life with a new name. The weird part is most such witnesses are often small-time criminals who made deals to testify in exchange for their freedom. This means that marshals now spend much of their time hiding and protecting criminals from other criminals.

Oh, the irony.

THE SECRET SERVICE

Founded right after the killing of Abraham Lincoln, the US Secret Service is the nation's second-oldest federal detective agency (the US Post Office is the oldest one. I know, weird).

Before Lincoln's murder, the president was protected by a patchwork system of Washington DC police, US Army soldiers, and occasionally hired detectives. In the aftermath of the first American presidential assassination, the US Secret Service was formed not only to protect the next president but also to combat a growing criminal problem that threatened the federal government—counterfeiting.

"Greenback" money was first issued by the federal government to pay soldiers during the Civil War. Prior to that time, the US government only issued gold, silver and copper coins. The early paper money was easily, and frequently, counterfeited, and the economy suffered as a result.

The Secret Service first began this dual mission in the age of telegraph and railroad, and they continue to grow into the cell phone and jet plane age, although hesitantly. To be honest, Americans have always feared the formation of a "secret police" the likes of which existed in Czar's Russia or the Kaiser's Germany. A force that spies on citizens on behalf of the government runs counter to many folks ideas of American democracy. Therefore, the Secret Service's powers of investigation were always quite limited.

THE AGE OF THE G-MEN

In the early twentieth century, the nation was faced with rapid and unpredictable changes. New technology, such as the telephone, the radio, powered flight, and the automobile, forever changed how Americans lived. Also, of no small import, the US government decided alcohol should be illegal, and a prohibition on all forms of booze was the law from 1920 to 1933.

Further complicating the situation, the stock market crash of 1929 brought on the Great Depression. Fewer Americans were able to make an honest living, and crime rates shot up nationwide. In fact, the problem of organized crime in the city of Chicago was so bad that the US Congress is said to have seriously considered sending in the Marine Corps.

The marines would have been a poor choice, as soldiers have no police training or detective skills to speak of. The Secret Service had its hands legally tied by Congress. And the local police were, as before mentioned, often corrupt and part of the problem. The need for a new, nationwide, law enforcement agency that couldn't be touched by the influences of corruption seemed obvious. Does the term "the untouchables" sound familiar?

Federal Government investigators, G-men for short, could pursue bank robbers that drove across state lines, racketeers who committed felonies by phone and take down criminal gangs that were getting rich on the sale of illegal liquor. This was the birth of the Federal Bureau of Investigations, or simply the FBI.

It grew from a small investigative office under the Department of Justice that had existed since 1908, and at first, its agents were not even allowed to carry guns. Often called “Treasury Agents” because they enforced the tax laws and banking rules of the Treasury Department, they were sent out to tackle the interstate criminal problems of modern America.

Unfortunately, they had a rather rough start. An outlaw named John Dillinger was one of their more notorious foes, and the early G-men were no match for him. For instance, in 1934, they learned Dillinger and his gang was staying at a hotel called Little Bohemia in Wisconsin. The resulting raid left one agent dead, another wounded, and two bystanders were shot in the crossfire (one dead, one wounded).

Oh, and Dillinger got away.

In 1935, J. Edgar Hoover was put in charge of the bureau by President Franklin Roosevelt. Director Hoover proved to be an able administrator. He reorganized the FBI completely, created the "Ten Most Wanted List," and generally professionalized the FBI. His early agents were mostly ex-lawyers with a sophisticated understanding of the law, and they were considered an elite crime-fighting force by the public.

However, as popular as they were in the movies, the G-men were very unpopular in law enforcement circles. Old city cops and deputy sheriffs often found Hoover's agents to be a bunch of arrogant know-it-all's. And these "out of towners" were seldom seen as brother officers, but rather as an intrusion on the local cop's turf. The presence of FBI men in a small town or big city was often a recipe for conflict with the police officers who knew the town best.

Mr. Hoover kept his job until his death in 1972, and boy was he a character. Outwardly moral and upright in all things, he was thought to be incorruptible, but power does corrupt. He was an intensely paranoid man who used his agents to spy on American politicians, presidents, and citizens. It is said he kept his job so long because every politician in Washington DC was afraid of the dirt he had on them. He also saw communist agents behind everything from the Brinks Armored Car robbery of the 1950s to the anti-war movement of the 1960s.

It is also rumored that Mr. Hoover was a closet transvestite. However, Susan Rosenstiel is the only witness to report that he cross-dressed, and she may not have been a reliable source. It is true he never married and never seemed to be interested in dating women (or men for that matter) so do with that what you will, fiction writer.

CHAPTER XII: MODERN POLICE

"This is the .44 magnum the most powerful handgun in the world, and it can blow your head clean off. Do you feel lucky, punk?"

-

Dirty Harry

In the United States, people generally have conflicting views about the police. Citizens want strong law enforcement to protect them and severe punishments for crimes as long as it's directed at someone else. However, when it's directed at themselves, well, attitudes change rather drastically. In times of social unrest and rising crime rates, this push-pull dynamic can change the way cops do their job in some very fundamental ways.

For example, in the early 1960s, *The Andy Griffith Show*, portrayed southern lawmen as friendly and benign. The image of the friendly sheriff who was only there to help epitomized how Americans generally believed police behaved. This image faded fast, however, when Chief "Bull" Connor ordered his officers to attack non-violent civil rights protesters in Birmingham, Alabama. Public opinion turned sharply away from lawmen as a result of this and other incidents, and that trend has continued. By the mid-1970's, that benign trust in the police was not a given.

Citizens took action, and things changed for law enforcement at the local, state and federal level. States started passing laws restricting police brutality and emphasized the rights of the accused. Several federal court cases, such as Miranda vs. Arizona (1966), ruled that police had overstepped their authority and imposed new restrictions. Thus, "Miranda Warnings," and other such practices, became a new part of police procedures.

However, as these needed reforms went into place, the crime rate steadily rose. Crime is a young man's game, and as the baby boomers reached adulthood, incidents of violent crime went up proportionally.

Against this backdrop, Hollywood created a new cop, Inspector Harry Callahan aka Dirty Harry. The movie Dirty Harry starred Clint Eastwood as an ultra-tough policeman who carried the biggest handgun he could find (size matters?). Harry took no crap from criminals or politicians and enforced the law—without always obeying it. The movie was action packed, provided a visceral thrill, and was quite successful at the time.

The other side of that coin, however, was Serpico.

Frank Serpico was an actual person who became a policeman for New York City in 1960 and did not enjoy a long career. Serpico ticked off just about every cop in New York by refusing to take bribes or to "shakedown" criminals. And worse than that, he broke the code of silence. Serpico made public his experiences with police corruption, testifying before the Knapp Commission in 1971. For his testimony, he received numerous death threats that probably came from fellow officers. Eventually, he resigned from the police force and moved to Switzerland for his own safety. A movie was made of his story, called Serpico, in 1973 starring Al Pacino and, like Dirty Harry enjoyed immense popularity.

The conflict between the Dirty Harry and the Serpico types is still ongoing. Legitimate questions are being asked, such as: At what point do cops need to bend, or even break, the rules in order to protect the public? And, at what point do the cops actually become a menace to the public they protect?

We now live in a time when police are under almost constant scrutiny. Intensive background checks are conducted on every police applicant, making law enforcement jobs very hard to get. Once hired, recruits are professionally trained and constantly reviewed. Every department now has policies and procedures regulating how police officers are expected to behave on the job and even when off duty.

Unfortunately, the "old guard" hasn't exactly died off as much as gone underground. An applicant may face a police interviewer who chooses to screen out folks he views as potential squealers. Likewise, a rookie may be purposely put into a small moral quandary by his seniors to test his reaction to a petty misdeed.

Naturally, this old guard seldom acts

with impunity anymore. Each department has its own internal affairs office to investigate allegations of police wrongdoing. These offices have the power to end a career or even send a fellow cop to jail. Naturally, no cop wants to be tainted by an internal affairs review, and just being called into that office can be the cause of much department drama.

Also, in this new millennium, cameras are placed everywhere from the squad car to the jailhouse, not only to get evidence of the criminal's actions but also to monitor the cop. A further, recent, development is the introduction of "body cameras" worn on the officer's shirt to record his entire shift. To add to the fun, into this environment of oversight and scrutiny comes the unpredictable nature of crime itself.

In a world where violence may be visited on a cop at any moment, a policeman may have to act quickly to stay alive. Will your character make the right decision in such a moment? Such dilemmas are hell on a cop but ripe fruit for any fiction writer.

Also, please keep in mind that not all departments have the same culture. I was paying attention to the news from Ferguson, Missouri in 2015, and I can honestly say I have never seen a department so poorly managed. Naturally, how professional or corrupt a fiction writer portrays a police department depends on the shape of the story the author wishes to tell.

POLICE LINGO

Like the military, cops have a language all their own. Much of it developed after the first police radio was installed in a Detroit squad car back in 1921. Cops must be clear and concise over the airwaves, but also once had to be a bit cryptic because they never knew who was listening. So, most departments used "ten-codes" at one time to confound the criminal with a police scanner.

Today's radios are digitally encrypted, so the ten-codes have been mostly abandoned in favor of "plain language." However, codes still linger on in cop-speak out of old habit. When spoken, they are pronounced like so: "Car Fifty-Four to Station. I'm going to be ten-thirty-eight on the corner of Lincoln and Halley."

Here is a short list of some popular ten-codes:

10-1—I can’t understand you
10-4—Acknowledgment
10-6—Busy, stand by
10-9—Repeat
10-10—Negative
10-14—Prowler report
10-15—Civil disturbance
10-16—Domestic disturbance
10-17—Meet complainant
10-20—Officer’s location
10-21—Call me by telephone
10-22—Disregard
10-23—Arrived at the scene
10-24—Assignment completed
10-25—Report in person
10-32—Man with a gun
10-33—Emergency (all cops stop talking and listen)
10-38—Stopping suspicious vehicle
10-39—Use light and siren
10-40—Silent run, no light or siren
10-41—Beginning tour of duty
10-42—Ending tour of duty
10-50—Accident

10-52—Ambulance needed

10-70—Fire

10-73—Mental subject (someone acting crazy)

10-78—Need assistance (Officers using this code can expect every cop in the area to come in a hurry)

10-89—Bomb threat

10-95—Prisoner in custody

10-123—I'm taking a bathroom break (no cop can use this code without getting razzed by every other officer on his shift).

Police use words to replace letters just as the military folks do. However, just to frustrate as many people as possible, they use a totally different set of words. To make matters worse; many of the words they use are the names of persons or places. So when an officer transmits something about Adam David Baker he can either be referring to a person or a license plate:

A—Adam	N—Nora
B—Baker	O—Ocean
C—Charles	P—Paul
D—David	Q—Queen

E—Edward
F—Frank
G—George
H—Henry
I—Ida
J—John
K—King
L—Lincoln
M—Mary
R—Robert
S—Sam
T—Tom
U—Union
V—Victor
W—William
X—X-Ray
Y—Young
Z—Zebra

Police also have some terms that linger from the "bad-old-days" of policing. These terms are seldom used anymore because the practices they represent are career enders, such as:

Throw Down Weapon—A gun or knife a cop carries that can't be traced. If the cop were ever to shoot an unarmed person, he would throw it on the ground at the crime scene next to his victim. This is not to be confused with a "backup weapon," which is an authorized extra gun a cop may carry for self-defense in case the issued gun fails.

Code Of Silence—The practice of refusing to report bad behavior on the part of fellow officers.

Street Justice—When a cop physically

beats a perpetrator, instead of or in addition to an arrest out of a personal sense of justice.

Shake Down—Stealing from criminals (After all, who are they going to tell, the police?)

MODERN POLICE GEAR

Gone are the days when cops were required to buy their own gun. Now, the police force will foot the bill for all of an officer's equipment. Police still carry clubs, usually in the form of a retractable steel baton worn on the belt. That belt also holds a semi-automatic handgun, two magazines of ammunition, walkie-talkie radio, can of pepper spray (mace), cell phone, case of disposable rubber gloves, small flashlight, taser, and two sets of handcuffs. The cop also wears a body armor vest under the uniform shirt and maybe a body camera pinned to the outside of it too. With all this gear it doesn't take a lot of writer imagination to see how uncomfortable a cop can be on a hot day, and back problems are a common policeman's complaint.

Police cars are designed for high-speed

pursuit. The back seat is a cage for locking arrestees in, and the passenger seat is usually taken up with a laptop computer and a GPS system. Also, a shotgun or assault rifle will typically be either next to the driver's seat or in the car's trunk with the first aid kit, evidence kit, road flairs and a dozen other items of an emergency nature.

POLICE RANKS

As with the military, police departments have a hierarchy of ranks. In general, they follow the military model and often wear similar insignia to the army's on their uniforms. The trouble is, every department is free to create whatever system of rank it desires and feels no need to be compatible with other departments.

Oftentimes, the larger the department, the more complicated its rank structure will be. A small town police department might have only four rank steps, whereas a department the size of Chicago or New York may have up to fifteen or twenty.

Some of the more common police ranks are as follows:

Rookie—*A cop just out of the academy. This term is usually unofficial, and his actual rank is "officer."*

Deputy—*This term is used mostly in sheriffs' departments. It's the equivalent of an officer. However, deputies have all the legal power of a sheriff and can "deputize" a civilian under emergency circumstances.*

Officer—*The majority of police are officers, uniformed cops with no supervisory authority.*

Corporal—*The most junior of supervisors.*

Sergeant—*The highest rank one can maintain and still be in a police union.*

Lieutenant—*The most junior management position within the force.*

Captain—*A middle management position, usually in charge of an entire shift.*

Major—*Sometimes called an "inspector," this is the senior management position in larger departments.*

Detective—*One must be a uniformed officer for a number of years before applying for this position. After obtaining the rank, detectives follow a separate career track from the rest of the force. However, they can rise through their own ranks to become "detective sergeants," or "detective lieutenants" and so on.*

Chief—*The highest career position within a department. Any higher position such as "sheriff" or "police commissioner" is a political position in the local government.*

Agent—*This term is preferred by the federal government for entry-level lawmen. For instance, the US Border Patrol is made up of agents who wear uniforms and behave like officers.*

Special Agent—*What is "special" about these folks is their ability to swear a witness, thus allowing them to record a "sworn statement" that will be admissible in court. This term usually is applied to federal investigators, such as the FBI or ATF.*

COP CULTURE

There are those who are meant to BE the police and those who are meant to CALL the police.

- Common cop expression

A cop's shift begins with a roll call in the briefing room where they are given all the pertinent information as was passed down from the last shift. The shift ends in the parking lot where the cop and his buddies talk about the shift's events and wind down from all the stress.

Naturally, there is strong camaraderie among police that draws them together as a close group, and there are also forces that push them apart from the rest of society.

Cops work odd hours that are out of step with the nine-to-five lives of most citizens. Cops also work a lot of mandatory overtime, and that can alienate them from wives and husbands. The divorce rate is high, and many of the marriages that do survive involve husbands and wives who work for the same department. For instance, I once met a police sergeant who had two ex-husbands working for her department, and she was dating another of the department's sergeants when I knew her.

Adding to the alienation, many people avoid cops for fear that they will get in trouble for something petty while others will draw uncomfortably close to a policeman because they hope to somehow gain favor with the law. Also, police officers almost never get called to see people behaving well. Their shifts are spent running from crisis to crisis, encountering people at their worst. A strong "us vs. them" mentality often taints veteran officer's perceptions, further alienating them from the people they are sworn to protect.

For these reasons, it's not uncommon for young policemen and women to find that after a few years on the job all their friends are cops. After all, who else can they trust?

Understandably, a cop is expected to give his all for fellow officers. If your character's partner is getting beat up by a gang of thugs, he better jump in the fight. If he gets beat up too, that's acceptable. But to hold back out of fear will alienate you from all other cops, and who else can you go drinking with?

This mentality can explain why the code of silence has been an especially tough thing to shake from the police world. In reformed departments, the practice is for one officer to say to another, "You need to report yourself to the captain before I go to his office on your behalf...You have an hour."

In unreformed departments, cops simply cover up each other's mistakes out of camaraderie. Policemen often refer to this as the "thin blue line" evoking the image of brave souls in blue uniforms forming a line against all that is evil in society. Because the line is thin, the loss of even one officer, for any reason at all, hurts everyone.

When a cop dies in the line of duty, officers tie a black ribbon over their badge out of respect. Police funerals are attended by representatives of every agency in the state, and woe unto the sorry department that doesn't send a representative in uniform.

The death of a cop will send a department on a frenzied hunt for the killer as almost no other crime can. The view is that a person who would kill a cop is a greater danger to the public. It is also felt that the rest of society can't possibly understand what cops go through to protect average citizens—so we protect our own like no one else can.

In this high-stress environment, police

burnout is a very common phenomenon. Many cops wash out in their rookie year, others switch careers in midlife (like becoming a writer perhaps), and of course, some are fired. As with the soldier, PTSD is a problem. The police suicide rate is consistently twice as high as the general population. Few make it to retirement and, on average, most cops who do only collect a pension for about five years before going to that great precinct in the sky. It seems many people have a hard time adjusting from being one who was the police to one who must call the police.

I recommend the book Emotional Survival for Law Enforcement: A Guide for Officers and Their Families by Kevin M. Gilmartin Ph.D. It is required reading at the Oregon Public Safety Academy, and it gives a good idea as to what kinds of stress cops have to overcome throughout their careers.

SWAT TEAMS

In the mid to late 1960s with the rise of radical groups, such as the Weather Men and the Symbionese Liberation Army, many departments concluded new methods of policing were needed. Many new officers at that time were also Vietnam veterans and wanted to put their experience to work. This led to the addition of a new kind of paramilitary police team. SWAT stands for Special Weapons and Tactics, and such teams are to be deployed when unusual situations overwhelm the traditional officer in a squad car.

Today, the new term is TERT, for Tactical Emergency Response Team, but the basic concept hasn't changed much since the early years. These teams are typically staffed with ex-military types who've completed their rookie year and try out for the new position. Team recruits attend specialized police training in small unit tactics and are considered to be the elite of the police force.

Typically, SWAT members work a patrol shift like any other officer until an emergency arises. When that happens, all the team members are called to the station—whether on duty or not. Quickly changing into tactical uniforms, they grab assault weapons and head out to deal with the crisis.

Fair to say, there has been some controversy regarding these teams. For one, they are very expensive to equip and train so they can be a strain on a department facing budget cuts. Also, the reliance on such teams has possibly made some average street officers reluctant to engage in situations where early action might have been critical, such as the Columbine High School shooting of 1999.

That being said, SWAT/TERT teams are also a source of departmental pride and a sign of status. They compete against other teams in state and regional competitions as a way of demonstrating a department's overall prowess, and much is made of the trophies they bring home.

When I was a deputy sheriff in Gaston County, North Carolina, there were three such teams in that jurisdiction. The Gastonia City Police, Gaston County Police, and the Sheriff's Office each had one, although it was widely recognized that three teams weren't needed to serve a population the size of that county. However, no department wanted to lose the status of having a tactical team.

UNDERCOVER COPS

It is not out of the ordinary for an officer to pose as a person attempting to buy drugs as part of a "sting" operation. And, as a minority of cops are women, it is also extremely common for a policewoman to pose as a hooker in an anti-prostitution sting at some time in her career. These can be considered brief escapades into the undercover world. Officers who go under for long periods of time are a different breed altogether.

The fact is, very few cops have the desire or the stamina to do such work. To go deep undercover means to abandon your family and friends (who are probably all cops) and join a criminal gang. An undercover cop can spend weeks or years living among criminals, collecting evidence while trying not to break the law themselves.

A living legend in undercover work is Billy Queen, a Bureau of Alcohol Tobacco and Firearms special agent who successfully penetrated the Mongols motorcycle gang in 1988. Queen spent years in the Mongols, almost totally out of touch with the law enforcement community he served. And, over time, he began to feel more affinity for the gang he joined than the department he worked for.

Eventually, Special Agent Queen came in and turned state's evidence on the gang's leadership, prompting several high profile convictions. Although Queen survived the assignment, his marriage did not. Nor was he able to return to the law enforcement community—he just couldn't fit in anymore. His book, Under and Alone: The True Story of the Undercover Agent Who Infiltrated America's Most Violent Outlaw Motorcycle Gang is a fascinating read and tells of the hard work and total dedication this kind of thing requires.

Instead of sending a cop undercover, it's often preferred to recruit a member of a gang as a police "informant." Informants are not cops and enjoy none of their comradely protection. These are criminals, usually offered a chance to reduce their charges in exchange for cooperation with the police. Occasionally, they are even paid by the police but still never entirely trusted.

POLICE POWERS

Officers of the law, naturally, have many legal powers ordinary citizens lack. They also have restrictions on those powers they must be constantly aware of. Now, please remember, although I will be discussing legal concepts, I am not a lawyer and don't pretend to be. If you find yourself in real-world trouble with a real police officer, I don't recommend you wave this book in the cop's face and say, "I don't need an attorney! I got everything I need to know right here!"

Such a story may not have a happy ending for you.

Also, please keep in mind, laws vary by state, so if you want to get very specific, you will need to look up the appropriate statutes. However, it is also true that there are some things that are almost universal in America. The constitution sets limits on public officials, and each state can only vary from that document by so much, so let us begin.

The power to detain is based on

"reasonable suspicion." For instance, if your character matches the description of a person the police are looking for; they can be stopped and questioned by a cop. Of course, they are under no legal obligation to answer the policeman's questions, but folks generally do anyway. If they say something incriminating, the cop can arrest them and must read their Miranda warning before asking anything else about the crime.

If the officer finds out, they've got the wrong person they must let them go. If the cop has no reasonable suspicion to detain someone but does so anyway, he is engaging in police harassment. A citizen's complaint of harassment will be investigated by the internal affairs office and could result in a reprimand for the policeman. Enough reprimands and the officer can get fired.

Although some states have such a thing as a "citizen's arrest," few encourage its use. Most citizens know far too little about the law to make an arrest and risk being charged with kidnapping if they bungle it. Law enforcement officers have not only the power but also the duty to arrest when they have "probable cause."

A police officer can make an arrest whether on or off duty, but without probable cause, she is opening herself up to trouble. Probable cause means the cop knows for a fact a crime has been committed, and the person they arrest is probably the cause of it. Maybe the officer saw the person commit the crime, or they may have several credible witnesses report that person to them. There may even be evidence of the crime they can trace to the person they arrests. But, without probable cause, there can be no arrest.

Keep in mind probable cause is not the same as guilt "beyond a reasonable doubt." A court cannot convict on probable cause alone. Therefore, a cop needs to gather as much evidence as possible to make a conviction likely. Witness statements and physical evidence are very helpful and the more the better, but regardless, a policeman can never take "fruit from a poisonous tree."

The "fruit from a poisonous tree" expression applies to evidence police obtain illegally. If a cop conducts an illegal search of someone's house, no evidence found in such a search will ever make it into the courtroom. Therefore, police are very careful to collect evidence according to the rules. To collect "fruit" illegally is to waste time and just opens the officer up to lawsuits.

Naturally, when people think of police searches they think of warrants. If a cop has probable cause, she can go to a judge and request a warrant to search a specific person's property for a specific piece of evidence. However, this is not always the way it goes down. Often the officer will just ask a citizen, "Can I search your car?" and if the person says "yes," no warrant is needed (and yes, citizens do have the right to refuse).

Also, if evidence is in "plain view" a cop needs no warrant. An example of plain view is a bloody knife in the middle of a public street. After all, it's not considered reasonable for a police officer to need a warrant when they are in a public place and the evidence is right in front of them.

Plain view gets murky, however, in less public situations. Say a cop is standing on the sidewalk and sees a man hit an old woman in the face. The man runs into a house and the cop chases him inside. In most states, the cop is considered to be in "hot pursuit" and is allowed to go into the house after the man. Once in the house, the cop naturally arrests the man for assault. But while putting on the handcuffs, the cop can't help but notice the bags of cocaine covering the man's sofa.

Plain view?

Yep, the cop had a legal reason to be in the house, so the cocaine is legal evidence. If the cocaine had been hidden under the sofa, perhaps our hypothetical policeman would not have seen it, and a search would not have been warranted, and the drugs never found.

The cop who will spend the most time thinking about correctly obtaining evidence is the detective. Charged with investigating crimes where the perpetrator is not obvious, detectives need to be able to spot small clues and properly exploit them. Often, only one piece of evidence exists to link the perpetrator to the crime. So a detective can hardly afford to have that thrown out of court due to a shady search.

A note here on fantasy vs. reality: in most fiction, detectives work on one case at a time. Oh boy, do they wish that was so, but it's not how it works.

Typically, a police detective has a load of cases weighing down her desk and is trying to solve several at once. Only in the instance of a missing child or an otherwise highly publicized crime will the detective put aside all her other work to pursue just one case.

USE OF FORCE

Perhaps there is nothing more controversial in law enforcement than the "use of force." Police brutality is not tolerated in this day and age, and when a cop must put his hands on a citizen, the reasons must be clear.

Use of force, put in the most general terms, is any action a cop may take, in regards to a citizen, to perform his duties. Thus, the lowest level of force is "officer presence," meaning the cop just stands there watching, and that alone discourages the criminal from doing wrong. Obviously, the highest level of force is a bullet in the head. In between are such steps as talking to someone, handcuffing them, or striking someone.

Cops are trained to enforce the law using the lowest level of force necessary to control the situation. In the ideal world, the citizen determines the level of force used against him by the way he behaves. A compliant citizen who submits to arrest should not be struck by a policeman. However, a citizen who raises a fist to a cop can expect to be hit in the process of arrest.

Any use of physical force by an officer will mean writing a report about it and, as cops hate to write, they often refrain from using force whenever they can. Deadly force is given even more scrutiny.

Police do not shoot people to enforce the law, per se. They may only use deadly force to protect themselves, or others, from death or serious injury. For instance, if a person attacks a police officer with a knife (a deadly weapon) the officer may shoot them in self-defense. Similarly, if a person attacks another citizen with a knife, the cop may shoot to defend that citizen. It is not the intent of the law that the cop suddenly becomes judge, jury, and executioner. He is simply acting to protect the innocent from the violent.

Keep in mind; the decision to use force is ALWAYS made under stress. In these scenarios, police have to make quick decisions based on incomplete information and mistakes happen. In a world where many people carry guns, a civilian who reaches into his belt in a fast and aggressive manner may find himself shot before he can touch his cell phone.

Incidents of deadly force will result in a cop turning in their weapon and being placed on paid leave while the internal affairs squad conducts a thorough investigation. The results of such an investigation can conceivably put a cop in prison for murder, and even if cleared of wrongdoing, the media attention and psychological stress can take quite a toll.

The movie cop who engages in daily firefights with the bad guys is strictly fiction.

FIREFIGHTERS, PARAMEDICS, AND OTHER FIRST RESPONDERS

Being a rescue worker definitely falls under the category of an adventurous profession. It's hazardous work with a high price for failure. Surprisingly, it is also a relatively new profession in the history of the world.

Volunteer fire departments, first organized in Philadelphia by Benjamin Franklin, started to gain momentum early in the country's history. Having a volunteer fire department may have been one step above the bucket brigade, but it was an important step. Of course, volunteer firefighters still exist today. In larger communities, they supplement the professionals who do the job forty hours a week.

Today, firefighters receive specialized training in their field and earn a state certification upon completion of an academy course. They become experts in chemical disasters, emergency rescue procedures, and first aid as well as basic firefighting.

Oftentimes, fire departments provide arson investigators to aid the police, and that itself is a full-time job.

Paramedics are a younger profession still. In the early part of the twentieth century, ambulance drivers were just drivers. Ambulances were called “meat wagons, ” and their only job was to drive a victim to a hospital as fast as they could.

It wasn’t until 1966 that things changed radically. A study titled: Accidental Death and Disability: The Neglected Disease of Modern Society showed that soldiers in Vietnam had a better survival rate than accident victims at home. Today, paramedics are highly skilled individuals who must undergo extensive training to receive their state certification. Some work for private ambulance services, and others for county agencies or even fire departments.

As with all professions discussed in this book, there is a strong sense of brotherhood/sisterhood among rescue workers. Even cops view them as part of their extended family. After all, if a police officer is hurt, they know who is coming to take them to the hospital.

Keep in mind; rescue workers face death and tragedy on a daily basis making it one of the highest stress jobs imaginable. Sadly, they also frequently suffer from Post-Traumatic Stress Disorder, just like a war veteran might. The more seasoned ones often develop a sense of "gallows humor" and can be heard making jokes only other rescue workers could find funny. This is an important coping skill because if you care too much, you just won't make it as a career rescue worker.

CORRECTIONAL OFFICERS

"We come from a dark history."

- Correctional Sergeant Ruvalcaba, Oregon DOC

In many ways, correctional officers are the "red-headed-step-children" of law enforcement. They lack any power of arrest but do have a lot of power over those already arrested. Also known as jailers, prison guards, correctional deputies, bulls, or screws, the only people who ever actually call them cops are the inmates.

Police, with the power of arrest, often look down on correctional officers as a lesser kind of cop and may refer to them as "cage kickers." But the truth is, I never met a policeman who wanted a prisoner riding in the back of his car any longer than he had to.

Sadly, it is only in the last fifty or sixty years that the public's demanded much oversight into how inmates are treated. In times past, it wasn't unheard of to punish inmates through beatings and other forms of abuse. For a feel of "the bad old days" of incarceration, I recommend The Green Mile or The Shawshank Redemption, by Stephen King. Mr. King obviously did his research and, credit where it's due tells some good stories.

In those bad old days, corrupt officers often profited from inmates by smuggling in alcohol or other vices for a price. Of course, such practices have always been forbidden, and a CO risks his career by even attempting this. In some cases, the officer can be risking his freedom as well and can be arrested for such infractions.

Incarcerated persons can spend as much as a year in a county jail, either serving their sentence for a misdemeanor or simply awaiting trial. If they are convicted of a felony, inmates are then taken to a prison run by the state government's department of corrections or, in some cases, a federal penitentiary.

Naturally, when a crime happens in a jail or prison, it must be investigated. Policies differ from agency to agency, but often the investigation will be handled by an outside investigative team. At the state level, it's usually the state police (highway patrol) who investigate crimes such as murder and rape within a prison. True, it's the prison's officers who will know the circumstances best, but no institution can tolerate the whiff of a cover-up in this day and age.

The correctional officer has some of the same skills as the policeman. He or she is expected to be able to defend themselves in a fight and will write reports after the fact that will be admissible in court. However, a CO also needs to be able to build respect with criminals and know how to talk them into compliance with the rules—because fighting every day is a recipe for burnout.

Whereas the street cop must make snap judgments about people he just met, the CO may see the same criminal every day for thirty years. In the course of a prisoner's sentence, the same officer may even meet the guy's family when they come to visit, and the CO may even be the one to call the family if the inmate dies of a heart attack before his sentence is up.

Officers in a prison build rapport with the folks they lock up, and there is often a grudging respect that develops. That being said, a correctional officer can still shoot a felon dead if he runs for the fence line. Prison can be an interesting place.

CHAPTER XIII: NON-TRADITIONAL LAW ENFORCEMENT

BOUNTY HUNTERS

Putting a price on someone's head induces all kinds of folks to come out of the woodwork to do their civic duty, and there is much history behind the practice. In America, rewards were typically offered by the state or federal government but could also be posted by private citizens. For instance, the railroad companies would frequently offer a reward for the capture of train robbers such as the James brothers.

The old west bounty hunter was everything from the professional gunslinger to the hick farmer who thought he could get lucky. Remember, these cowboys had no legal authority, and they were not "cops" in any sense. But they did have the power of citizen's arrest and, as long as they didn't exceed that authority, were within the limits of the law and could be called the "good guys" or at least the better guys than the bad guys they pursued.

A good movie on the subject is *The Outlaw Josey Wales,* starring Clint Eastwood. Bounty hunters chase Jose across the west, but few stand a chance in this classic film based on the book *Gone to Texas* by Forest Carter. This brings up a point worth mentioning: the higher the reward, the more your character must put life on the line to collect it.

THE PINKERTON MEN

Allen Pinkerton was the greatest detective of his time. By that I mean, he was successful in not only solving cases but also in starting the first well-known detective agency in the United States. Pinkerton's company was once arguably the most famous private security firm in the world. Raymond Chandler's hard-boiled detective character, Philip Marlowe, even refers to them as his competition as late as 1939 the novel, *The Big Sleep*.

The Pinkerton National Detective Agency was founded in 1850, and its motto was "The eye that never sleeps." Allen

Pinkerton and his men began solving crimes for hire in Chicago and, at the time, were the only real detectives around. Most police departments kept no detectives on staff, and it was common practice to use private detectives as contractors. In fact, Sherlock Holmes in Arthur Conan Doyle's books was such a contract detective and not an actual policeman at all.

As the country expanded west, so did the Pinkerton men. They chased the James Gang, in the employ of the railroad companies, guarded payrolls, and served as bodyguards for any who could afford them.

The pay of a Pinkerton detective was usually higher than that of a proper lawman, and they probably didn't mind rubbing a cop's face in that little fact every now and again. Guns were purchased at their own expense, but they could afford the good ones. The movie *3:10 to Yuma,* starring Russell Crow, features the Pinkertons of that time in action.

The Pinkerton Company often took contracts that tested the limits of what private security can do in a democracy. For instance, they were hired by the Federal

Government to spy on the Confederate Army and found many contracts with industry as "strike-breakers."

As they protected factories from rioting workers or spied on trade unions meetings, they gained a nasty reputation. To this day, many union folks despise the name "Pinkerton." However, the name has also lost a lot of its prestige due to changes in the security marketplace. The company still offers detective services but is just one of many such firms today.

BAIL BONDSMEN

The modern equivalent of a bounty hunter is often thought to be a bail bondsman. They are licensed through their state government, but they do not actually work for the state and are thus considered private business persons.

Say a shady character is arrested but doesn't really want to stay in jail. The magistrate who heard the cop's report also set the suspect's "bail:" an amount of money that, once collected by the court, will be held until the trial date. While "out on bail" the arrested person walks free. When that person shows up for trial, all the money is refunded to him. Of course, at the trial, it will be decided if the person is guilty or innocent, and they will either go free or go to prison.

Now, let's say your shady character doesn't have enough money to pay his bail but has some cash just the same. In that case, he can call a bail bondsman. The bondsman will come to the jail and visit with some papers for your inmate to sign. Your shady character gives the bondsman about twenty percent of the bail's total, in cash, and the bondsman pays the rest. If your character shows up for trial, the bondsman gets all his money back and also keeps the twenty percent.

After all, this is a business, not a charity.

But let's say your character skips bail and doesn't show up for trial at all. Now the bail bondsman is ticked! The only way he can get his money back is to get your shady character's butt back in jail. Oh, those papers that were signed? Basically, they give the bondsman the legal authority to come after the character.

And bondsmen have scary legal powers over bondholders. They can go anywhere they have reason to believe the offender is hiding and drag them to court. Remember, the shady character signed and agreed to all of this back at the jail and there's no going back now.

Keep in mind, however, that bail bondsmen in the lawful execution of their duties still aren't cops. Police do not treat them as equals, and if they leave their state, they have no license to work under. Some states, like Oregon, don't even allow bail bonds to begin with, so working there can get a bondsman in a lot of trouble.

When I was a North Carolina deputy sheriff, I once locked up a bail bondsman I had known for years. The poor gal left North Carolina, where she was licensed, and went to get a fugitive in Kentucky, where she wasn't. The fugitive surrendered without a fuss, and then his relatives called the cops to report a kidnapping. Local police arrested the bail bondswoman at a highway rest stop and released her "victim." I greeted the bail bondsmen when she was extradited back to

North Carolina to stand trial for the kidnapping. What happened next I don't know (my National Guard unit sent me to Iraq that month).

BODYGUARDS

These are not cops, but characters often encounter them in a similar way. You might consider them mercenaries who specialize in personal protection. They are usually big folks that look intimidating and can handle themselves in a fight (sound familiar). They are serious about doing what they are told by their employer and often know the law on self-defense quite well. If your character attacks them, they won't hesitate to fight.

Professional bodyguards are often veterans of the military and frequently work for corporate executives. They go through extensive training at private schools specific to personal protection. A professional such as this will know how many exits are in the employer's hotel, where the nearest fire extinguisher is, at least three safe routes from the hotel to the employer's place of work, as well as the names and faces of many of the employer's associates. Such bodyguards are usually armed with handguns and pepper spray. They wear body armor and typically carry radios or cell phones. All of this gear is hidden under a smart business suit, but the bodyguard's demeanor often gives them away just the same.

Unlike corporate head honchos, high-ranking criminals rely on trusted friends to protect them. Such a friend will be a fellow thug who has been with "the boss" for years and knows his habits, friends, and enemies very well. This crook will not be as thorough or refined as the executive's other professional protector. But, on the other hand, he will be extremely loyal and willing to break the law to protect his boss whereas the corporate bodyguard may not.

SECURITY OFFICERS

You see them in shopping malls and you're probably not too impressed. Sometimes overweight and often looking bored, they're mostly watching for shoplifters and lost kids. Many security officers work for private companies who contract out to factories and warehouses. In most instances, these folks are just there to satisfy some insurance policy's requirements, and they actually don't do much. The term "security theater" often applies to these efforts; meaning it's all just a show to make the place look like it's protected. Security guards on such contract jobs are usually unarmed and will not present a serious challenge to a determined criminal.

But they will call the cops in a heartbeat.

Now, to every rule, there is an exception. The same companies that provide the security officer to the used car lot often have another, more elite department. Former cops and soldiers are often recruited to work at nuclear power plants or defense installations as security guards. These guys and gals are well paid and physically fit. They carry serious firepower and are authorized to use it.

Frankly, it can be funny as hell if your characters mistake one type of security officer for the other.

VIGILANTES

The most famous vigilante the world has ever known never actually existed—Batman. Armed with super fantastic gadgets, a black costume, a cape, and an unlimited supply of money, he fights crime and saves the city—again, and again, and again. True-life vigilantes aren't so sleek.

A vigilante is any person who, without authority, takes the law into their own hands. They hunt down people with or without any actual evidence. And they often beat or murder those who they believe to be criminals without any pretense of a trial. Naturally, cops view these folks as a menace and are not likely to work with them on a case or summon them with a spotlight when the city is in danger.

Sadly, in American history, we've had lots of vigilantes. They were called lynch mobs, and they were a disgrace to all that is American. Groups of "upright citizens," enraged by some alleged crime, stormed out into the streets, grabbed someone who they believed to be guilty (usually using skin color as evidence), and hanged them by the neck from some tree. They would even storm jails, lynching a person on the night before his trial, and that put the real lawmen in one hell of a position.

Writing about a cop who stands before a lynch mob and says "no" can be challenging, to say the least. Not only is your character out-gunned and outnumbered, but these can be the same "prominent citizens" the police rely upon in normal times (Are you the sheriff? Who votes around here?). Doing the right thing is important to most readers, and some brave lawmen and women in our history have stood up to the mob. Characters in this position need to be smart, as well as brave, to save the day.

A vigilante story can be quite an imaginative exercise if you are going for the caped-hero type. Such stories are usually set in fictional worlds that only resemble our own (come on, find the actual Metropolis or Gotham on a map, I dare you).

If you're creating such a world out of whole cloth, you need not worry about how real law enforcement agencies would behave. If, however, you're setting your tale in our reality, expect conflicts with the cops as well as with the criminals, and there'll be no help if your hero gets in trouble. An example from the golden age of comics would be the Green Hornet, whom both the cops and the criminals believed to be an outlaw.

Writing about a cop with a meddlesome caped vigilante in his town can also be good stuff for a writer. The Caped Cuckoo can be a bumbling interference as the cop tries to solve a case, but what if the nut's onto something as well? Or perhaps the vigilante may be the menace the cop must track down and arrest…before someone else gets killed.

PRIVATE EYES

The private investigator is not a cop. He or she has no connection with actual law enforcement and is really just an ordinary citizen like the bail bondsman. States require a private investigator to have a license, which is only given after they pass a criminal background check and/or a state exam.

Many of these detectives are ex-cops, some retired and some fired.

As stated above, Allen Pinkerton was as such a detective, and his company's eyeball logo coined the term "private eye." The "private" part is important, as these people go to great lengths to protect the privacy of their clients.

Private investigators are hired for a number of reasons. An insurance company will have some on staff to find out if someone is defrauding them. A husband or wife may hire one to discover if their partner is cheating. A parent may hire a private investigator to find a runaway child. All of this work is perfectly legal and may involve no actual crime on anyone's part.

The line gets blurry, however, where great story possibilities emerge. What if the guy who cheats on his wife is also a big-time drug dealer with a gang of thugs to protect him? What happens, for instance, when the husband your character is following is murdered, and the private investigator becomes the suspect?

These are the seeds of great private eye fiction by the likes of Dashiell Hammett who wrote *The Maltese Falcon*, and Mickey Spillane who gave us *I, The Jury*. Incidentally, Hammett was a private detective for years before he started writing. I recommend any writer wishing to do "hard-boiled" detective fiction to read his works or watch the movies made from them.

Without the support of a large police force or any actual authority, the private eye has only wits and street smarts to survive in a cold, cruel world full of danger and adventure.

CHAPTER XIV: FOREIGN POLICE

LAW ENFORCEMENT AROUND THE WORLD

Where do I begin? Let's just say there's a lot of variety out there, folks.

Most countries have a national police force instead of the hundreds of local departments like we do in the USA. This means issues of jurisdiction seldom arise, but there is also less local control over the force.

It's true that the regular police of Great Britain are not usually seen with guns. They do, however, carry radios and those radios are used to call "Armed Response Units."

Imagine a bunch of bored cops, with guns, sitting in the back of a van, and drinking tea. When a police officer calls for an ARU they dump the tea and rush to the scene. And they are prepared to use deadly force to protect the public and maintain law and order. So yes, they have guns in Britain, you just don't usually see them.

Happy to say, the British have a very professional force that is, in many other ways, similar to American police departments. Less developed countries, however, can be a bit more interesting.

I was once told a tale by a fellow US soldier who had direct experience with the Iraqi Police. The story went like this: It was 2003, and the US Army had orders to stop looting in Iraq. My buddy and his small team were walking through Baghdad with an interpreter. Suddenly, a bunch of locals came running up to the US soldiers to report a bank was being robbed. The soldiers surrounded the bank, and their interpreter talked the robber into surrendering. Sounds like a happy ending, right? Now all the US soldiers had to do was call the cops.

The robber was lying face down in front of the bank when the Iraqi Police finally showed up. The American soldiers told the cops what happened, and the Iraqi authorities took the man into custody. Which meant the first thing the Iraqi cops did was to start kicking the ever-loving crap out of the robber as he lay defenseless on the ground.

As the robber screamed and clutched himself in agony, my friend the soldier shouted at the police, "Hey, stop! You can't do that!"

To this, the Iraqi Police replied, "Oh, so sorry. You are right. You arrested him...you kick."

Darn polite chaps those Iraqi cops.

In short, if your characters run afoul of the law in some undeveloped, non-democratic country, the rules of the modern American lawmen just don't apply. Brutality and corruption can be quite open. In fact, in most cases, the Iraqis I talked to in 2011 would not go to the police at all. Instead, they preferred to call a tribal leader, their sheik, in times of trouble. Once the sheik knew all the details, he would typically send some cousins to handle the matter in a very vigilante sort of way.

THE FUTURE OF LAW ENFORCEMENT

Science fiction has given us stories like *Bladerunner* and *Judge Dredd*, where cops are little more than assassins for the law. Conversely, we also have numerous predictions that private security may one day replace police forces. Already, some states are experimenting with privately run prisons and corporate police forces. I personally consider privatizing law enforcement a very bad idea because companies established to make a profit already have a goal above public safety in mind and will frequently sacrifice the one for the other.

In the future, anything is possible. But the current trend is for more and more professional police forces with higher tech gadgets and a strict adherence to the law. The ever-present cell phones with their camera features are the latest tool for holding officers to high moral standards, and only a dumb cop will ignore them. In fact, the smart cop will enlist the aid of the public in documenting events that can lead to a criminal's conviction.

Will we ever get rid of police corruption? Only if we replace living breathing cops with robots. A good cop will find himself in bad situations and sometimes make the wrong call. A bad cop will look for opportunities to make bad decisions and do his damnedest to get away with it. Human nature is what it is.

How corrupt are the police really? Depends on the time, the place, and the officers involved. As a fiction writer, you're free to tell the story the way you want. As a member of the law enforcement community, however, I do ask that you keep in mind that most people who become police officers are in the job because they hope they can do some good in the world, and more officers are a credit to the profession than otherwise.

PART C: INTELLIGENCE PROFESSIONALS

I could tell you...but then I'd have to kill you.

- The world's oldest spy joke.

CHAPTER XV: HISTORY OF ESPIONAGE

A FEW WORDS FROM YOUR HUMBLE AUTHOR

As I stated at the beginning of this book, I am a retired, US Army, Counterintelligence Special Agent. As such, I am subject to the National Security Act of 1947 and Title 18 of the US Code. In laymen's terms, that means I have to watch my darn mouth, so I don't go to jail.

As such, I was required to submit this work to the Department of Defense for a security review. They did so, and I was assigned the case number DOPSR #14-S-

0558. Whenever you encounter a black line in the text, know that's the kind of thing they do.

Sleep safe, America.

We now return to our regularly scheduled writer's guide.

HISTORY OF SPYING

"I regret that I have but one life to give for my country."

-- Last words said by Nathan Hale, famous spy.

There is nothing new under the sun, and espionage is no exception. Think about it; has there ever been a time when a ruler didn't want to know what his neighbors were up to in the next kingdom over?

The Bible's *Book of Joshua* even refers to Hebrew spies slipping into the town of Jericho before the Israelites attacked. In that story, these cloak and dagger men of God made friends with a prostitute. She gave them the information they needed in exchange for her family's safety, and everyone lived happily ever after (eh?).

In *The Art of War*, Sun-Tsu states, “It is essential to seek out enemy agents who have come to conduct espionage against you and to bribe them to serve you. Give them instructions and care for them. Thus, double agents are recruited and used.”

Like I said, some things never change…

However, as old as it is, spying can be hard to research because most countries don’t want it known they’ve ever done that sort of thing. “Spying” is a bad word in our language. Nobody likes a spy, and they are only considered heroes after they’re dead—and only if they spied on the right side as history remembers it.

Remember Benedict Arnold?—spy, and General Washington wanted him dead.

Despite George Washington’s loathing for Arnold, the father of our country often used intelligence agents himself. In fact, his best network, the “Culper Ring,” was, so secret historians only found out it existed when a trunk of letters was discovered in 1939!

Culper Jr. and Culper Sr. were the

code names of two agents whose real names were Woodhall and Townsend. They worked in British occupied New York City and reported enemy troop movements directly to Washington.

Still, many more Americans are familiar with another Revolutionary War intelligence agent, Nathan Hale. Mr. Hale's fame derives from the fact he was caught and executed. This lends credence to the fact that successful agents are the ones whose identities are not revealed until after their death (by natural causes).

Naturally, Washington knew the British were spying on his army as well. To that end, he created a false supply document (never told a lie, my butt) during the Valley Forge ordeal that he let slip into British hands. The document led the British to believe Washington had more troops to feed than he actually did, so the British chose not to attack and the nation was saved.

Washington abandoned his spy network after the war was won, and no effort was made to form a national spy agency thereafter. Of course, that is not to say there were no spies; they just didn't work for an official organization. It is doubtless, American embassy staffs weren't above gathering information through less than obvious means in foreign countries. And in the American West, "scouts" advised army commanders on the disposition and activities of native tribes. This was spying on an ad-hoc basis. These were merely local diplomats and army officers taking initiative to collect information that was of immediate use to them professionally.

Continuing this model, Lincoln hired the famous detective Alan Pinkerton to report on the rebels' activities. The funny thing was, Pinkerton (code-named "Major Alan") was surprisingly bad at the job. He got consistently outfoxed by confederate ruses that led him to believe the enemy had thousands of more troops than they actually did. This led to timid US Army action, which resulted in a Union defeat during the Peninsular Campaign of 1862. It seems being a great detective doesn't necessarily translate into success as a part-time intelligence agent.

Having a full-time agency of trained people dedicated to only this one job is a relatively modern phenomenon. This is because having a national spy agency is, in effect, announcing to the world that you will be spying, and for some reason, most folks don't like to hear that from a neighboring country.

Every nation in the world views espionage as a crime within its borders. Therefore, no nation can afford to admit they make a practice of spying, lest they admit to a felony. The press may publish a story about some nation or other "spying," but the nation itself will recoil from using that term. In fact, I wish to make clear that nothing in this book should be taken as confirming or denying that the US is currently involved in criminal activity of any kind!

Therefore, American intelligence professionals do not "spy" on others. Oh, no, they merrily "collect information." To collect information sounds as harmless as collecting butterflies (unless you're a butterfly). And the term is so sanitized it doesn't even suggest the use of clandestine means. Thus, the intelligence agent separates himself from some of those nasty spy notions of criminal espionage and can step at least one foot into the light.

It's the bad guys who are the spies, and that's our story and we're sticking to it.

EARLY INTELLIGENCE AGENCIES

With semantics out of the way, let's begin our discussion of modern intelligence agencies. The British were actually the pioneers in this endeavor when they formed "Military Intelligence Sections Five and Six" in 1889, more commonly referred to as MI5 and MI6 today.

Overseas intelligence collection is the responsibility of MI6. While MI5 conducts counterintelligence operations to thwart foreign spy efforts within the United Kingdom. Britain had the world's largest empire at the time MI5 and MI6 started and having an organized network of intelligence professionals proved vital to that empire's survival. This was especially true in troubled colonies like Ireland where frequent insurgencies threatened to topple the Royal government.

It was, in fact, the Brits who schooled

the Americans in the arts of organized intelligence collection in the middle of the last century. Their motives, of course, were quite clear; Britain was fighting for its very survival and needed to get its allies up to speed.

Having an intelligence apparatus already in place proved to be a great asset in World War II. They ran rings around the Germans, and that's no small part of the reason why Britain managed to remain free after most of Europe had fallen. An example of such skill was the genius of MI5's "Double Cross System."

Early in the war, MI5 managed to capture a few German spies, withhold that news from the public, and more importantly conceal it from Berlin. The unit responsible for this program was known as the "Twenty Division" (or XX in Roman numerals—double cross, get it?). The captured spies were kept in a manor house in the English countryside and were treated rather well, as long as they continued to send messages to Berlin. That's right, MI5 wanted them to communicate with their bosses using the same radios they brought with them in the first place. Of course, Twenty Division's agents wrote the script for every word they spoke.

Sending the occasional bit of real information masked the mountains of deceptive information the Nazis received. When Berlin asked the captive spies what they could do to make their jobs easier, the answer was always, "send more spies."

Soon a gaggle of German agents were parachuting into Britain, only to be caught the second their feet hit the ground. Only a few unlucky enough to have their capture reported in the newspaper were publicly shot as spies. The rest lived out the war comfortably, sending false information to their masters.

Sadly, as good as the British were, the Russians were better. Before World War II even started, the Soviet Union worked hard to develop spies in the west.

Perhaps their greatest coup was the recruitment of the "Cambridge Five." Cambridge is the home of one of Britain's best universities, and, like many other employers, it was there the Russians went looking for bright young men of good education.

Five students, who were active in the British Communist Party, but hadn't actually joined yet, were recruited. All of them chose to spy for ideological reasons, and each went on to get jobs in the British government. The master of them all was a man named Kim Philby (yes, a men named Kim) who was employed by MI6 itself and fed the Soviets every scrap of information Britain learned from 1940 until his defection in 1963.

Philby's greatest achievement was to prevent MI6 from aiding the German resistance. He feared if the Germans managed to assassinate Hitler only the war in Western Europe would end, leaving the Soviets to fight alone. So, without British aid, the German resistance tried anyway. They famously failed to kill Hitler, on July 20th, 1944 and were rounded up and put to death.

Kim Philby even worked with American agents from time to time as Britain shephearded along its cousins from across the pond. America, it seems, was slow to enter the intelligence game.

As mentioned above, there were ad-hoc intelligence rings in early American history. However, we did have the smallest sliver of an intelligence service at the dawn of the twentieth century. Both the army and navy had intelligence personnel who were charged with creating American codes, breaking foreign codes and occasionally doing targeted intelligence collection.

If you recall, in the movie *Raiders of The Lost Ark*, Indiana Jones was hired by men connected with army intelligence to find the ark. This is realistic to the extent that it was not unheard of for the army to hire Americans to collect specific information while traveling.

The FBI attempted to get into the game using the angle that espionage is a crime, and thus a law enforcement matter. This did not go smoothly as J. Edgar Hoover's ego chafed the Pentagon's brass. The military and the FBI often worked at cross-purposes, and when political leaders wanted specific intelligence, they still tended to rely on the older methods. In fact, that is the reason President Roosevelt sent a lawyer on a secret mission to Europe in 1940.

William J. Donavon (Wild Bill) was a

Medal of Honor recipient of World War I who practiced the law in the interwar years. He was well traveled, intelligent and had the complete trust of President Roosevelt (despite his being a Republican). In his secret travels, he met with Britain's Prime Minister Churchill who discussed with him the notion of an American intelligence agency. Donovan thought it a pretty good idea.

During World War II, the US formed its first actual intelligence agency with Donovan at the head called the Office of Strategic Services. The OSS was part of the US Army, and Donovan was given the rank of brigadier general. Most OSS personnel were recruited from army ranks, but the organization also included civilians like Julia Child (yes, the "*French Chef*" of 1970's TV fame).

Despite a smattering of civilians, the OSS was seen as a military unit, meant to support regular military forces on the battlefield. Advisors from MI5 and MI6 helped train OSS men in tradecraft at a secret facility in Canada, called "Camp X." From there, agents were sent to Europe and the Pacific to collect information on our enemies.

Incidentally, Edgar Hoover didn't like the OSS either, and despite World War II's pressing needs, insisted intelligence work was exclusively a law enforcement responsibility. After much wrangling, an agreement was reached whereby the FBI was given free rein to collect intelligence within the USA and, for some odd reason, South America while the OSS operated everywhere else.

At the conclusion of the war, Donavon was given a nice pension and put out to pasture. Shortly after that, the OSS was disbanded after news of a sex scandal (possibly invented by Hoover) reached President Truman's ear. Still, the war taught America valuable lessons about the need for a professional, full-time intelligence service.

It also taught America of the need for an air force, and a unified department of defense. All these things were rolled into one bill called the National Security Act, which Truman signed into law in 1947.

THE COLD WAR

"From Stettin in the Baltic to Trieste in the Adriatic, an iron curtain has descended across the Continent."

- Winston Churchill, 1948

After World War II, the nations that fought to make the world free had some serious disagreements about what that freedom meant. To the Soviet Union, establishing communist governments and creating a buffer zone against future western invasions seemed a pretty good idea. However, other Allies seemed to think differently.

After such an exhausting task as defeating the Axis, neither side was in the mood to settle their differences on the battlefield right away. But the lack of direct warfare didn't preclude more quiet rivalries. For the next forty-three years, the world's superpowers squared off in "proxy-wars" for control of developing nations. Actual shooting took place in countries such as Greece, Korea, Vietnam, and Afghanistan.

Somewhat subtler were the Soviet sponsorship of communist revolutions in Cuba, Nicaragua, Angola, and Cambodia. The USA returned the favor by sponsoring coups in Iran, Guatemala, and Chile.

Even in more stable countries such as East and West Germany, the two giants worked to gain the upper hand in the battle for information. The disposition of military forces on both sides was also constantly studied for any hint of aggression that could lead to war. In a very real sense; we owe a debt to the intelligence agents on both sides who kept nuclear war from breaking out over false information or simple misunderstandings.

Fiction writers of the cold war era made a lot of money from spy novels. The most famous being Ian Fleming, who, by the way, served in MI6 during World War II before writing the *James Bond* novels. His first novel, *Casino Royale,* portrayed the life of a secret agent as glamorous and exciting, full of mystery, exotic travel, sex, and danger. The book was an instant best-seller and prompted a wave of imitators. And, for perhaps the first time in history, the spy was the hero in popular culture, and not the villain.

Frankly, I often wondered how an ex-intelligence man like Fleming could get away with writing such a book. After all, secrets and the methods of discovering them must be well guarded. Could Her Majesty's Government have prosecuted Mr. Fleming for treason? It turns out the answer is, "no," because there was almost nothing in the *James Bond* novels that had any relation to real life spying.

A more realistic novel of that time is *Tinker, Taylor, Soldier, Spy* by John LeCarre. Mr. LeCarre worked for the British Foreign service before turning to writing, and his books are nothing if not well researched. I will also be so bold to put a plug in here for my book, *Red Coat Running*, which was inspired by my experience in the ██████ doing ██████████ for the army.

The good news for writers who wish to explore the Cold War is that much of it has been made public. The collapse of the Soviet Union let loose a flood of information previously unavailable to the public.

Similarly, US intelligence agencies routinely de-classify information once it is no longer considered of value (typically 25 years after the fact).

Also, it's not unheard of for retired intelligence professionals to write books on the subject.

In 1979, former CIA Agent Kermit Roosevelt (son of President Teddy Roosevelt) published *Countercoup: The Struggle for the Control of Iran*; in which he spilled the beans about the CIA operation that put the Shaw on the throne in 1953 (which worked out SO well for the USA in the long run).

To be frank, the Cold War had so much happening in terms of intelligence history this book cannot even begin to do it justice. Every method of intelligence collection ever thought of was tried by one side, the other, or both in that period. Ironically, the game went on for so long; the players even began to know each other by first name. A grudging respect developed between the rivals, and occasionally they even helped each other out.

A story is told that a young KGB agent

was to be murdered by ████████████████████. American agents discovered the plot and decided it was in nobody's interests to see this idiot dead. So they grabbed the kid off the street and threw him in the back of a car. The CIA guys then drove the hapless spy straight to the Soviet embassy with the understanding the reds now owed the Americans a favor.

Yep, the cold war was a strange time.

CHAPTER XVI: THREE LETTER AGENCIES

ALPHABET SOUP

After the National Security Act of 1947 became law, the US finally had a peacetime intelligence agency. Well, to be frank, it had several. The most famous would, of course, be the Central Intelligence Agency. But the act also created the National Security Agency (NSA), and the Bureau of Intelligence and Research (INR). These agencies plus the already existing US Army Intelligence, US Navy Intelligence, US Air Force Intelligence and the FBI were the geneses of the post-war American intelligence community.

Nor did the creation of agencies stop in 1947. Over time many more have been created, each with their own intelligence niche to fill. A short list includes the Defense Intelligence Agency (DIA), the Defense Security Service (DSS), the National Geospatial-Intelligence Agency (NGA), the National Reconnaissance Office

(NRO), the Office of Intelligence Analysis (OIA), and the Bureau of Intelligence and Research (BIR).

With such a potpourri of bureaucrats snooping around, it's not surprising; they occasionally bump into each other. Each agency has its own field of expertise, but each is also is in competition for their slice of the federal budget, and this can make for some interesting situations. A movie that makes great sport of these rivalries is *The President's Analyst* starring James Coburn. Even if you are writing a serious work of fiction, know that the intelligence community is not always filled with good neighbors and that film does a good job of mocking our darker side.

THE CENTRAL INTELLIGENCE AGENCY

To be clear, the CIA is the big fish in the American intelligence pond. I have some experience with "The Company," though not of a professional nature. Instead, my CIA background comes from family connections.

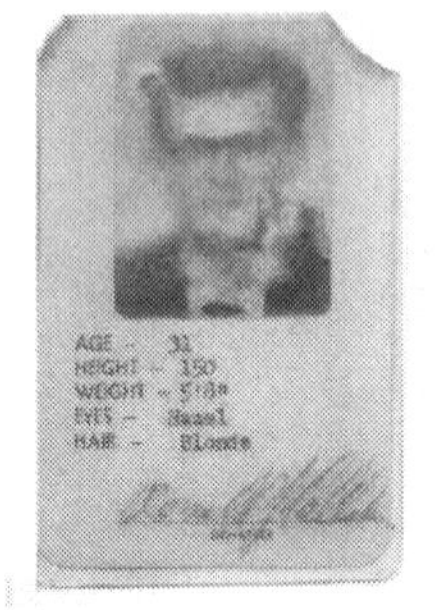

In 1970, my father, Ronald J. Callahan was a CIA agent. And the family kept his ID card as a service memento. I **don't** recommend you try to get access to a CIA office today using this ID! After all, even the government updates things from time to time. However, proof of its authenticity as a US Government document can be found by noting Ronald Callahan's height is listed as 150 and his weight is 5'8." Oh yea, the CIA…they know all.

My dad took the gig because he was tired of his day job—programming computers with punch cards. He felt lucky to get the position. However, he did not enjoy a long career with "the agency." First, he was trained at "the farm" which was ████████████ at the time, and then he shuffled paperwork at the CIA's main office in Langley, Virginia while ██████████████████.

Then came the day when the CIA gave

Agent Callahan his first permanent assignment—to work at their new computer center in Pittsburgh, Pennsylvania. Ronald resigned almost immediately, yet somehow the agency has managed without him.

Besides the resignation of the occasional agent, the CIA's job is also made harder by the very act of Congress that created it. The CIA is not allowed to collect intelligence on Americans and, therefore, cannot legally conduct operations within the USA. For this reason, they often have to coordinate with the FBI when espionage crosses our borders.

This means if you want CIA characters spying within the USA for your story you will either have to invent a compelling nefarious reason or have the CIA subordinate to the FBI in some way.

OTHER "THREE LETTER" AGENCIES

Like jumbo shrimp, military intelligence is a contradiction in terms.

- World's second oldest spy joke.

Although the OSS is no more, the US Army still collects intelligence and has agents to do it as was the case when ██████████. Also, there are Navy, Air Force, and Marine branches of military intelligence that ultimately report to the Defense Intelligence Agency. Some of these agents wear military uniforms, and others do not, depending on their mission.

However, it is generally true that these agents are military personnel. They have a military rank and are performing an assigned duty like any other soldier. Although considered the low men on the intelligence totem pole, military personnel often find some of the more juicy information simply because they're on the front lines, facing the enemy up close and personal.

But civilian agencies also permeate the battlefield in other ways. The main offices of the NSA, for example, are located on Ft. Meade, Maryland, and as you may guess, they create the codes used by the military.

The National Security Agency is charged with protecting our nation's communications systems and is probably the geekiest member of the intelligence community. They are considered the masters of cyber warfare and do their best work while sitting in cubicles.

In my early military career, I served at Fort Meade standing guard at the gates to the NSA campus. Here's a crazy story that went around that place concerning an old hotel and the KGB. Back in the 1970s, the KGB was said to have used a dummy company to build a hotel right next to the NSA headquarters. The Russian thinking was probably to listen in on out of town agents with hidden microphones when our guys had to travel to the main office. Unfortunately for the Russians, the NSA found out about it by ███████. So, before the hotel even opened, the NSA bought the building and just left it unoccupied.

Meanwhile, the NSA faced another security threat—tourists. Nerdy Americans were making pilgrimages to the NSA, taking pictures, and asking employees a lot of awkward questions. So the NSA solved this problem by turning the old hotel into The National Cryptological Museum. For a couple of bucks, tourists can now walk right in and see declassified "spy stuff" on display while taking a tour lead by a retired NSA staffer.

Personally, I think creative thinking like that speaks well of any government agency.

The National Reconnaissance Office creates maps. Which sounds boring, but it was the NRO that discovered the nuclear missiles being placed in Cuba in 1962. The U2 plane that took the original pictures of Soviet missiles was on NRO assignment when flying over Castro's island. The map that resulted went straight to President Kennedy and prompted thirteen of the most intense days of the Cold War period.

Much about the Cuban Missile Crisis has been de-classified, and I recommend the Kevin Costner movie *Thirteen Days* for anyone interested in high-level intelligence fiction. The Cuban Missile Crisis was the closest this planet ever came to a thermonuclear holocaust so we would rate the NRO as at least somewhat interesting.

FEDERAL BUREAU of INVESTIGATION

The FBI belongs in Part B and Part C of this book because it straddles both the law enforcement and intelligence world. Since espionage against the US is a federal crime, the G-men have the responsibility of conducting counterintelligence operations against enemy spies.

Also, since the terrorist attacks of 9/11, there has been a greater emphasis in the FBI of working to prevent the next attack. Such a pro-active approach necessitates the collecting of intelligence on America's adversaries at home and abroad. To do so, the FBI must procure warrants and conduct themselves as cops while at the same time keeping secrets from the enemy as intelligence agents. To say the least, it's a fine line the FBI walks, and it's not without controversy.

CHAPTER XVI: INTELLIGENCE CULTURE

"Our successes are secret. Our failures are all over the daily news."

-Common intelligence professional's lament

The American intelligence community has a unique culture all its own. Unlike the military or police, there is less of an esprit-de-corps, and rivalries between agencies and individuals can be quite intense. The number one rule is, "He who produces the most is rewarded the most." By production, I mean the collection of information of value to our superiors.

As mentioned above, the US's collection of three-letter-agencies has some overlap in their areas of expertise. Similarly, within agencies, there is overlap between departments and teams. If this is your career, and you're a go-getter, you need to get the information first and stay in front of the pack at all times. Sharing information with incompetent or treacherous co-workers can get your sources blown (revealed to the world) and put you out of business. In this environment, sharing of information is done reluctantly and only to the extent the leadership insists it is necessary.

Since the terrorist attacks of 9/11, a greater emphasis has been placed on cooperation between intelligence agencies, the military, and law enforcement. "Fusion centers" have been created where members of the law enforcement and intelligence communities share information to prevent the next terrorist attack. How successful this effort has been is meat for the imaginative fiction writer to chew on.

Keep in mind that for intelligence people, paranoia and distrust are part of the job description. The US has been betrayed by its own people in the past, so there is constant vigilance within the ranks to weed out those dirty foreign spies and American traitors. Since the success of an agent's career, as well as his or her personal survival, depends on the ability to keep things to themselves, trusting people is just not part of the mindset. Also, know that the intelligence community is somewhat isolated from the rest of society simply because its members can't talk about their work problems with their friends or families. It can be a hard thing coming home to when you can't even tell your wife what kind of day you had.

However, they also honor each other's sacrifices. In the lobby of the CIA headquarters in Langley, Virginia, there is a display of over one-hundred stars. Eighty percent of the stars are gold and bear the names of fallen agents. Twenty percent of the stars are black and represent fallen agents whose names are classified.

INTELLIGENCE TERMS

Like every other profession, people who work in intelligence have a language all their own. Unlike the military or police, these terms did not evolve out of a need to be understood over a crackling radio or anything like that. In fact, the terms began as deliberately cryptic yet over time have entered the common vernacular anyway.

Agent—*One who acts on behalf of others. Typically this is a government employee but the term can also be used to describe an informant.*

Asset—*Someone who gives information to an agent.*

Burnt/Blown—*To be revealed as an agent.*

Brush Pass—*To pass an object to another person as you walk past them in such a way as to avoid discovery.*

Compromised—*To have your cover put in jeopardy of being blown.*

Counterintelligence—*The act of preventing intelligence from being collected. This usually mean using detective skills to uncover an enemy spy.*

Cyber CI—*The new frontier of counterintelligence and intelligence collection alike is the digital world. Amazing amounts of information pass over the internet every day and* .

Dead Drop—*An old-school method of secretly passing information by leaving documents in a hidden place for another to find later.*

Handler—*Once a spy is recruited, he or she will be assigned a "handler" to manage their espionage.*

Honey Pot—*An attractive person who uses sexual enticement to get intelligence from someone.*

Humint—*Short for Human-Intelligence and refers to collecting information from people.*

Imint—*Short for Image-Intelligence; refers to analyzing photographs for intelligence value.*

Mole—*A traitor within an intelligence organization.*

Polish—*To disguise one's self.*

Off the reservation—*When an agent goes "off the reservation," they are no longer obeying the rules that restrict their operations.*

Osint—*Short for Open-Source-Intelligence; refers to collecting information in overt ways such as reading foreign newspapers.*

The Company—*Early in the cold war this was a cryptic nickname CIA employees used for their agency. It is not at all cryptic anymore and is instead a kind of inside joke.*

Tradecraft—*The skills an intelligence professional uses in the field.*

Spook—*A nickname for anyone connected with the intelligence community.*

Source—*A person, place or thing that provides information.*

Sigint—*Short for Signals-Intelligence; refers to information gained through* ▇▇▇▇▇▇▇▇▇▇ *or by intercepting radio communications.*

Sexpionage—*The use of sex to gather intelligence information (honey pot).*

Wet Work—*Work that involves killing people.*

METHODS OF ESPIONAGE

The most closely held information maintained by intelligence operatives are their "sources and methods." In this way, they are much like newspaper reporters who have been known to go to jail for refusing to reveal their sources.

"Methods" refers to the way one works with one's sources who provide our information. Naturally, I cannot reveal any methods used by our American intelligence agents or our enemies would shut us down…but I can discuss methods used by our enemies.

By enemy, I mean folks who wish to commit espionage against the US. They range from rogue states like North Korea to terrorist groups like Al-Qaeda. Even nominal allies, such as Israel, have been known to spy on the US (a man named Pollard is currently doing life in a federal prison for just that). With spies seeking out American secrets from all directions, we must train our people to be on the lookout for their dastardly schemes. Therefore, it is actually encouraged for US agents to talk about how they operate.

Every soldier in the US Army receives an annual briefing on enemy methods of spying (Army Regulation 381-12). This briefing is meant to undermine foreign collection efforts and make the US Army less vulnerable to spying. What follows is information out of that same, *unclassified*, briefing.

Please also keep in mind that when an intelligence professional uses the phrase, "I can neither confirm nor deny that," people often take that for a "yes." People are often wrong. It means just what's stated and nothing more. I am neither confirming nor denying whether or not the US uses the following methods, so let us begin.

Recruiting American citizens to spy for foreign powers is a common enemy espionage method. It's simply much easier to recruit an American intelligence professional to turn traitor than it is to break into the CIA building at Langley in a black ninja costume (something I really don't recommend you try).

Enemy spies prefer to find an American sympathetic to their cause. Ideological recruits are generally easier to handle, more motivated to get the job done and cost little to no money. Such was the case with Julius Rosenberg who spied for the Soviet Union because he truly believed in communism. There has been a lot of controversy over the case of Mr. Rosenberg who was accused of giving the Soviets atomic secrets in the 1940s and 50s. At the time of his execution (and that of his wife as well), there was a loud movement protesting his innocence. However, the FBI has since declassified information gained from cracking the Russian's "Verona" code that leaves little doubt Mr. Rosenberg and his wife spied for Moscow. Not only did the Rosenbergs go to their deaths for the cause, they never received any payment for their clandestine services from the KGB.

Aldrich Ames was not so ideological. He was a CIA agent who moonlighted for the KGB and for that he was well compensated. In 1985, Mr. Ames went through a messy divorce and was in need of some extra money. Making matters worse, his girlfriend (and future wife) had expensive tastes. His solution was to sell Top Secret information to the Soviets. He received a sum between two and four million dollars over the course of an eight-year career as a KGB spy, and he is now serving a life sentence in a federal prison lieu of a pension.

Robert Hansson worked for peanuts comparatively, receiving only about $30,000 a year for a double agent career that spanned twenty-two years. He was the FBI's chief of counterintelligence, which means it was his job to find enemy spies within the US—and if he had pointed the finger at himself he would have saved everybody a lot of trouble. Spying for the KGB gave Mr. Hansson a sense of importance, and he was basically in it for the thrill.

Seduction can also be used to turn someone into a traitor, such as in the case of I Lonetree. Corporal Lonetree was stationed at the US embassy in Moscow in the early 1980s. His Russian girlfriend, Violetta Seina, enticed him into divulging classified information, which she passed on to the KGB. This KGB "honeypot" then used the fact he had already screwed up to blackmail him into further acts of espionage. Lonetree received a fifteen-year prison sentence, and Miss Seina, if that was her real name, has not been seen since.

As you can see from the above prison sentences and executions, it's the traitor who takes all the risk. The enemy spy who handles the spy takes all possible precautions to avoid being caught themselves; after all, they have their career to consider. The enemy handler seeks to avoid police surveillance by meeting with the traitor in as clandestine a manner as possible. Often the handler will meet the traitor in a neutral country to receive information and deliver payment.

Also, the spy handler may "fly a false flag" so the traitor doesn't even actually know who he is really working for. The traitor may think they are British when the spy is actually Russian. This serves the double purpose of persuading the traitor to work for "the good guys" while further concealing the handler from exposure when the traitor is caught and interrogated.

If you want to see a good spy movie that touches on a lot of these concepts, I recommend *Spy Game* starring Robert Redford. In the film, you see Robert Redford recruiting Brad Pitt as the enemy might recruit a traitor, but he uses him as a CIA agent. You also see Redford's character working against the CIA as a mole would—but for the right reasons. In short, the film gives its audience the kind of visceral thrill readers want in good spy fiction. And by keeping close to actual practices, the movie seems real to the audience, even if it's not entirely accurate.

SECRET DEVICES

Secret devices are famously a part of spy action movies. Watches that hide laser beams and pens that double as detonators are familiar to audiences the world over. In fact, many audiences have come to expect such paraphernalia in their spy fiction. Do such devices actually exist and are they really used?

The answers are yes...and no.

Today, you can find sunglasses with hidden cameras or pens with microphones simply by shopping online or in specialty stores. I even encountered a selection of these toys on sale at a street market in Baghdad. The problem with using such gadgets is they identify you as a spy. Face it; no one would possess such a thing if they weren't up to something sneaky. In the grand scheme of things, it is best not to put yourself under suspicion no matter the advantage of some device. Heck, most intelligence agents don't even carry a gun for fear it would expose them to suspicion, let alone a laser-beam watch!

It is true that briefcases that contained hidden compartments and pens that fired bullets were made in World War II for use by the OSS. It is also possible that some agencies invest money in a few specialty devices today. However, it was rare to unheard of for an agent to have used any of that stuff in World War II, and today there is simply no need to have a camera hidden in a bow tie when everyone carries a camera in their cell phone.

Using an "off the shelf" gadget, like a cell phone, is much less likely to arouse suspicion and will usually work just fine anyway.

INTELLIGENCE LAW

"James Bond, like all "00" agents, has a license to kill."

--Ian Fleming

There is no such thing as a license to

kill, and laws against that kind of behavior apply to intelligence agents as much as to everybody else.

In fact, most professionals do everything they can to avoid killing as murder investigations constitute unwanted attention. Such a scandal can not only end one's career but terminate the source of whatever information your agent was trying to get in the first place. Also, with each scandal that hits the papers, the US intelligence community finds itself under more and more legal scrutiny.

Does that mean assassinations are pure fiction? Unfortunately no, foreign spy agencies are still believed to engage in this behavior as when Alexander Litvinenko was killed in 2006 with polonium-210 (not an over-the-counter poison). The US, however, is forbidden to assassinate by Executive Order 12333. That being said, the line between illegally murdering a person and killing an enemy combatant can get blurry when your war has no front lines as in the 2011 death of Osama Bin Laden.

When I attended the US Army Counterintelligence Special Agent Course, weeks were spent learning intelligence law before any of the tradecraft was covered. Lawyers from the army's Judge Advocate General Corps taught law classes and were very in-depth. Subjects of discussion included the National Security Act of 1947, Title 18 of the US Justice Code, The Uniform Code of Military Justice, US Army Regulation 381-12, and the Bill of Rights. Why's the army giving its counterintelligence agents all this attention to legal matters?

Well, it's a long story.

The short version is that after the abuses of the Nixon administration, Congress took a long look at the US intelligence community. Among other things, the Church Committee of 1975 revealed the army had sent undercover agents to monitor American citizens at protest events. Naturally, this revelation proved highly unpopular and spawned a new era of congressional oversight that continues to this day.

Not only are US citizens protected by these laws but "US persons" are as well. A US person is anybody who is legally within the United States or can reasonably be assumed to be legally in the United States. For the intelligence community to snoop on people in the US, they must first get a warrant like any policeman would have to. As most of these requests for warrants are prompted by classified information, special federal courts exist to hear these cases (FISA Courts). The FISA courts generally frown on the US Army's requests unless US Army personnel are involved as the army has no jurisdiction over civilians. Typically, it is the FBI that conducts espionage investigations within the US.

If your fictional agents are somehow "above the law," be advised that anyone who aids them could end up in jail. More likely your rogue agents would seek to circumvent the law by finding loopholes or by abusing some kind of discretionary authority so they can get cooperation from law enforcement. Such a veneer of legitimacy will make it more plausible that your protagonists do not need to fear the police.

Of course, in fiction, you can do what you want. Going all out with an illegal intelligence activity in the US can make for a great story. Your characters may even report to the president if you like. However, they may well leave a trail of bodies as they have to kill every newspaper reporter or police detective they encounter.

With the threat of exposure by the press or arrest by the FBI, looming over your character's head, you can easily ramp up the tension in any spy novel when characters go "off the reservation" within the US.

Of course, one must keep in mind US laws do not apply overseas. Actions your fictional agents take in foreign countries will be under far less scrutiny and they can [illegible] without nearly as much paperwork.

SECURITY CLEARANCES

When someone first applies for a job with an intelligence agency, they also must apply for a security clearance. Many forms are filled out requiring the applicant to give the story of their lives in excruciating detail.

The military version of this application is called an SF-86 and is available online for your entertainment.

The paperwork, once submitted, is given to a background investigator who is expected to do a thorough job, checking to ensure every detail is true. Naturally, some agencies go further than others. When I applied for a job with the Secret Service, men in suits and sunglasses went so far as to knock on my neighbor's doors and ask a lot of questions. When I came home from work, all my pals wanted to know if I was in trouble.

I wasn't in trouble, but I still didn't get the job—bummer.

The conclusion of all this scrutiny is the granting of or denying of, a security clearance. All government information is categorized to determine how public it should be. Thus, only persons with a security clearance should be allowed to see "classified" information. Even then, a person must have a "need-to-know" concerning the particular information involved.

For instance, a CIA agent working in

Europe might have access to information on Europe but not South America. If she wanted to see a South American file, she would not only need the right clearance level but would also have to prove her need-to-know that specific information to her superiors.

The classification system can be broken down as follows:

Un-Classified—*Information that is available to the public.*

Sensitive—*Information that is available to the public, but is meant to be kept discreet as it might be prejudicial to national security. Leaking such information can result in a reprimand by one's employer.*

Confidential—*Information that would cause damage to national security if publicly disclosed. A criminal prosecution is an option for the intentional leaking of this information, but it's more likely to get a person reprimanded by the agency that employs him.*

Secret—*Information that would cause serious damage to national security if publicly available. People's lives may depend on keeping this information guarded, and criminal prosecution is likely for intentionally leaking it to the public.*

Top Secret—*Information that would cause grave damage to national security if made publicly available. As this is the most guarded of information, it is also the most likely to get a person criminally convicted for leaking it. Prosecutors can seek the death penalty in cases of espionage and are likely to do so for this level of treachery.*

Special Compartmentalized Information—*This is an add-on to the other, already existing clearances granting access to higher levels of information when the situation requires. For example, an agent may have "Secret with SCI" clearance.*

Classifications above Top Secret—*There are no publically acknowledged clearance above Top Secret. As a fiction writer, you are free to invent one, and you won't be the first.*

CODES

Naturally, one of the most damning things a spy can be caught with is a codebook. Not only would that compromise him, but it would allow his enemies to decode messages from other spies as well. Still, codes are a valuable way of keeping secrets.

So what's a spook to do?

The answer is to have a copy of *Tom Sawyer* by Mark Twain, on hand. Assuming the spy's handler has the exact same copy of the same innocent book, coded messages may look like this: 44-12, 18-3, 26-1. To decode the message, they would go to page 44 and look for the twelfth word, then page 18 and look for the third word, and so on. This way, if police find the spy's message, it represents nothing but a bunch of numbers and is useless to them unless the cops know which exact copy of what book to use as the key.

And if the spy is caught with a copy of *Tom Sawyer*, it only reveals their taste in literature.

THE INTELLIGENCE PROCESS

Intelligence, like alcohol, must go through a process before it is potent enough to have any effect. It starts with the "customers." These customers can be political leaders, military commanders or government bureaucrats. Customers generate lists of questions they want the intelligence community to answer for them, and these lists are known as Primary Intelligence Requirements.

Agents take the PIRs and go shopping for answers. Using the various methods agents collect raw data that is relevant to the PIRs and report it to their agencies. The agencies will give the raw data to analysts who sift through it all and try to form a cohesive picture. The analysts then make the information available to the customers. The customer does not need to know how the information was obtained and is usually just happy to have her question answered. The customer then uses the report to make decisions that affect governmental and military policy.

This process is so smooth and

seamless nothing ever goes wrong, ever, ever, ever.

A FINAL WORD FOR WRITERS

Well, writer, that's it.

If you found this book short, you're right, it is. As no book on such a wide swath of subject matter can be comprehensive, I didn't intend to try. Instead, I simply hoped to get you off to a good start.

Understanding the basics is critical to knowing where to begin your own research, and it keeps you from going down the path of bad assumptions. To learn more, you can, of course, surf the internet or go to the library. However, I also recommend you do some research in the form of first-hand experiences.

Naturally, I don't recommend you do a four-year hitch in the marines just to write one novel. But you can contact your local American Legion or Veterans of Foreign Wars Post and ask to interview someone who has been there and done that.

You can also arrange a "ride-along" with your local police. Ride-alongs are where you sit in a police car with an actual cop on patrol and observe her at work for a shift. You can get chatty with the officer, build some rapport, and learn all kinds of things about how your local department operates.

You may think the intelligence world is a bit harder to crack and you'd be right. However, intelligence agencies have acknowledged they need to open up on some level to the public. Most have Public Affairs Offices you can contact online or over the phone and possibly arrange an interview or at least get some printed information. It's in their best interests to portray their agency in a good light to the taxpayer, and they will do their best in that regard.

If you are new to writing, I would like to make another recommendation: join a writer's group!

A writer's group is made up of about three to six writers who agree to read and critique each other's stuff. Let's face it, we frequently look at our own work and see only what we expect to see. The critique process allows others to see what we actually wrote and give helpful advice on how to make it better.

Writer's groups can be found online or at many colleges and universities. You can also just settle down and form your own group with like-minded friends. Either way, it's the dedication each member brings that makes such a group successful or not. Each writer should do their best to help everyone in the group succeed.

That's how our band of brothers and sisters rolls.

I want to wish you all the best in your writing endeavors. In the end, the only way to become a good writer is to start out as a bad one and just keep at it. Don't get discouraged by rejection; we've all had buckets of it. If writing is your passion, keep at it!

The only way to fail at it is to not try.

Regards, Clayton J. Callahan

Recommended Reading for Military Matters

Osprey: Men at Arms series: Roman Centurions 31 BC~AD 500D'Amato, Raffaele—Osprey Publishing—Oxford—2012

Osprey: Men at Arms series: Republican Roman Army 200~104 BC—Sekunda, Nicholas—Osprey Publishing—Oxford -- 1996

Henry V—Shakespeare, William

The Three Musketeers—Dumas, Alexander

The Mercenary—Pournelle Jerry—Baen Books—1988

Hammer's Slammers—Drake, David—Nightshade Books—1983

The US Army Ranger Handbook: Sh 21/76—Red Bike Publishing—2010

The Defense of Duffer's Drift—Swinton, E.D—Renaissance Classics—2007

The Lost Fleet series—Campbell, Jack—Ace Books—2006~2010

The Four Feathers—Mason, AEW

Recommended Viewing for Military Matters

Master and Commander: the Far Side of the World—Weir, Peter—20th Century Fox—2003

Full Metal Jacket—Kubrick, Stanley—Warner Brothers—1987

An Officer and a Gentleman—Hackford, Taylor—Paramount—1982

Cops—Langley, John & Barbour, Malcolm—CBS Television—1989

Apocalypse Now—Coppola, Francis—Zoetrope Studios—1979

Dr Strangelove—Kubrick, Stanley—Columbia Pictures—1964

Strategic Air Command—Anthony Mann—Paramount Pictures—1955

The Guardian—Davis, Andrew—Buena Vista Pictures—2006

Black Hawk Down—Scott, Ridley—Columbia Pictures—2002

Beau Geste—Wellman, William—Paramount—1939

Enemy at the Gates—Annaud, Jean—Paramount—2001

Defiance—Zwick, Edward—Paramount Vantage—2008

Michel Collins—Jordan, Niel—Warner Brothers 1996

Recommended Reading for Law Enforcement Matters

Much Ado About Nothing—Shakespeare, William

Brother Cadfael books—Peters, Ellis—Marrow—1978

Guards! Guards!—Pratchett, Terry—Harper Torch—2001

Oliver Twist—Dickens, Charles—1837

The Adventures of Robin Hood—Pyle. Howard—1883

The Big Sleep—Chandler, Raymond—Alfred A. Knopf, Inc.—1939

The Maltese Falcon—Hammett, Dashiell—Orion—1930

I the Jury—Spillane, Mickey—E.P. Dutton—1947

Emotional Survival for Law Enforcement: A Guide for Officers and Their Families—Gilmartin, Kevin—E.S. Press—2002

Under and Alone: The True Story of the Undercover Agent Who Infiltrated America's Most Violent Outlaw Motorcycle Gang-- Queen, Billy—Random House—2006

Accidental Death and Disability: The Neglected Disease of Modern Society—National Academy of Sciences—1966

Recommended Viewing for Law Enforcement Matters

Arsenic and Old Lace—Capra, Frank—Warner Brothers—1944

Silverado—Kasdan, Lawrence—Columbia Pictures—1985

True Grit—Hathaway, Harry—Paramount Pictures—1969

The Fugitive—Davis, Andrew— Warner Brothers—1993

The Outlaw Jose Wales—Eastwood, Clint—Warner Brothers—1976

3:10 to Yuma—Mangold, James—Lionsgate—2007

Dirty Harry—Siegel, Don—Warner Brothers—1971

The First 48—Kim—A&E—2004

Bladerunner—Scott, Ridley—Warner Brothers—1982

Dredd—Travis, Pete—Lionsgate—2012

Recommended Reading for Intelligence Matters

The Bible, Joshua 6:1-27

The Art of War—Sun-Tsu

Army Regulation 381-12 (U)

Countercoup: The Struggle for the Control of Iran—Roosevelt, Kermit—McGraw-Hill—1979

Tinker Tailor Soldier Spy—LeCarre, John—Penguin Books—1986

Recommended Viewing for Intelligence Matters

Spy Game—Scott, Tony—Universal Pictures—2001

The President's Analyst—Flicker, Theodore—Paramount Pictures—1967

Thirteen Days—Donaldson, Roger—New Line Cinema—2000

The Falcon and the Snowman—John Schlesinger—MGM—1985
(*At one time people who were involved in various areas of intelligence were actually prohibited from seeing this movie.*)

Sneakers—Phil Alden Robinson—Universal Studios—2004

OTHER BOOKS BY CLAYTON J. CALLAHAN

The works of Clayton J. Callahan can be found wherever e-books are sold. All are influenced heavily by his professional experiences and you can see for yourself how weaving fact into fiction creates a new reality for the reader to enjoy.

He can be reached at his blog at

claytonjcallahan.wordpress.com

Clayton Callahan has made his living principally in the "uniforms and guns" professions. He is now writing fiction professionally and has works have been published by Double Dragon Publishing, Broadsword Books and World Castle Press. He lives and writes in the Portland, Oregon area.

Made in the USA
Middletown, DE
07 December 2018